The City of Hartford 1784–1984

Published by the Connecticut Historical Society with the Support of Society for Savings

The City of Hartford 1784–1984

An Illustrated History

By Ellsworth Strong Grant and Marion Hepburn Grant

Contents

Library of Congress Cataloging in Publication Data
Grant, Marion Hepburn, Ellsworth Strong
The City of Hartford 1784–1984
Includes Index
86-071682
ISBN 0-940748-91-6

Foreword

The year 1986 is a fitting time to publish a revised edition of Ellsworth and Marion Grant's book about Society for Savings and Hartford. This is a year that marked the return of Comet Halley. In our more immediate environment, this is a year, along with 1985, when both Connecticut and Hartford formally celebrate their 350th anniversaries. This is the year in which Society for Savings could have celebrated the attainment of a century and two-thirds of corporate life.

In a way, much has happened regionally and locally in the seventeen years since this book first appeared. Connecticut lost some of her vitality and then regained it, moving once again into an enviable economic position. So too, the City and the Greater Hartford area went through some setbacks before making impressive recoveries. Society for Savings endured some difficult years, but now finds itself much bigger and even healthier than it was in 1967. Our physical presence, through one business form or another, now reaches into fully half the states of the Union. As measured by assets, we are this year more than twice two times as big as we were on our 150th anniversary. We have become a publicly-owned institution.

In another way, very little change has taken place in the course of what, after all, is only a sixth of a century.

Pratt Street does not really look much different, people still matter most in our business, and bankers still smile in the presence of good customers. Like the complicated path of some great comet, it all sometimes actually seems to be pretty predictable.

We at Society champion Hartford because it is a great place to be. It is a city at the forefront of insurance, manufacturing and banking. It boasts ethnic and religious diversity, a spirit of innovation, a rich mixture of arts and architecture, a location along a great river, and a tradition of caring for humankind.

The Grants are well-known area natives who have produced numerous books and films on Connecticut history. They have retold Hartford's past for the benefit of our future.

Society for Savings was founded by citizens to help people, and in that spirit, we are proud to support the publication of this book as a way of telling Hartford's story to all.

Elliott C. Miller
President
Society for Savings

Introduction

Every history is either his or her story. This is *our* story of Hartford.

His Story

Though born in Wethersfield and raised in West Hartford, I consider myself a citizen of Hartford. I worked downtown for nearly 20 years, I belong to a Hartford church, and I have been involved for half a century with many of the city's organizations.

Moreover, as a descendant of the founder, Thomas Hooker, and of John Barnard, a ship captain who lived on Buckingham Street, my roots are deep. My father and grandfather and two of my uncles spent their working lives running, respectively, a factory, laundry, restaurant and department store. Both my parents graduated from Hartford High School.

All of this helps to explain my attachment. But there is much more. Situated as it is halfway between Boston and New York, Hartford in many ways is unique. Its proximity to the Connecticut River made it a thriving port, and the fertile soil on both banks produced a bounty for the early English settlers. They learned to grow corn and tobacco from the peaceful, land-loving Indian tribes. The happy combination of good crops close by a marine highway resulted in generations of hardy farmers and enterprising merchants. They laid the foundation for bottom-up government and established a tradition of independence and self-sufficiency.

Steady growth and adaptation to change have kept this old city young in spirit. Sure, there have been pauses and reverses, but the city has never lost a sense of forward movement. Just look at the different kinds of wealth that have been created over 350 years—from farming to shipping and merchandising, to insurance and manufacturing, land development, and most recently to communications and high technology. For its size Hartford is one of the nation's highest producers of goods and services.

Continuity amid change is another characteristic of Hartford. Besides the handful of physical landmarks to remind us of our past, the old work ethic and other solid values that inspired our forefathers and mothers are still alive. The city has been blessed, in every generation, with imaginative leaders who have not only kept their businesses growing and created many new jobs, but who have shown concern for the community's well-being.

As a result, Hartford can boast of having a remarkable variety of public institutions and facilities for health and welfare, education, the arts and recreation—many of them the first of their kind.

As the capital of Connecticut, Hartford enjoys a special kind of dignity and status. It is a pretty little city, compact, manageable and vibrant. Seen from the air or from the highways leading into it, Hartford offers a breathtaking spectacle, with its cluster of skyscrapers close by the river.

Her Story

We were a family of six children . . . three girls and three boys. When we were growing up in Hartford, our father delighted in taking us on tours of the city and surrounding areas . . . and our mother delighted in taking us on tours of Europe. Because he was a surgeon at a time when doctors were expected to stay close to their sick patients, Daddy could never be more than an hour's drive away from Hartford Hospital. As a result, he became an expert at touring in microcosm. He taught us, too, to enjoy traveling in our own backyards . . . to really see what was right under our noses. In the process, he told us stories . . . stories about Hartford history and the fascinating people who made history in this city.

Story-telling is essential to human social continuity. In primitive tribes (and in our family) parents and grandparents are the "tellers of tales" . . . recounters of the important stories that give the next generation a special identity. This gives them, during their own sojourn here on earth, the opportunity to live meaningful and purposeful lives.

As a native of Hartford, I am fascinated by the fact that the residents of this city represent practically all of the world's nations, cultures, religions and races. Our pluralistic society is poised on a space-age frontier. Most of the companies in which we work are multinational. The goods we purchase in our stores are grown or fabricated in all parts of the globe. Even our terrestrial home's place in the mysterious universe is constantly being reassessed by modern science. Yet we are held together in common community and our spiritual and material health and prosperity continue to be nourished and sustained by that historic, yet modern vision of creating here on the banks of the Connecticut a truly good city.

Yes, we love Hartford . . . past, present and future. Its spirit has never been just "make do" but always "do better." And in our story we have tried to capture its essence.

Marion and Ellsworth Grant
July, 1986.

Hartford in 1817.
Oil on canvas.

The City of Hartford

From the beginning in 1636 the founders of Hartford were determined to run their colony with a minimum of interference from the mother country and Massachusetts Bay. In view of their religious conservatism and intolerance, they were surprisingly innovative politically, as they formed a government whose authority derived from the people rather than a distant monarchy. Thomas Hooker's famous sermon asserted that "the choice of public magistrates belongs unto the people, by God's own allowance." It was a revolutionary concept that inspired the Fundamental Orders, the first written constitution in the world. It planted here the seed of democracy that would grow and flourish in the years to come and give Connecticut the right to call itself the Constitution State.

In 1783, as the 13-member states of the new American republic returned to peacetime pursuits, Hartford faced a political and economic crisis. Although before the Revolution it had been a bustling river port, the township depended mainly on farming. Its boundaries extended as far west as Farmington and, to the east across the Connecticut River, encompassed East Hartford and the future town of Manchester, altogether an area of 86 square miles. Most of the population of around 5,000 still resided in the town between the west bank of the river and Asylum Hill. They were simple farmers, shopkeepers and artisans accustomed at the 9 o'clock ringing of the church bells to drinking their last glass of cider, raking up their fires and retiring to their beds.

The insatiable demand for provisions by the troops of General Washington and the French allies had left the state virtually impoverished, while during the war its ports were commercially idle. Hartford's merchants and sea captains desperately wanted to restore the city's once prosperous maritime trade. They began to reopen their warehouses and ready their vessels, but they were up against both external and internal obstacles. Only a tiny fraction of the goods coming to Hartford were in Connecticut-owned bottoms; most were being imported, at much higher prices, in ships from Boston and New York. Furthermore, the British began dumping goods on the American market as part of a strategy to dominate overseas commerce. Finally, the business leaders felt thwarted by the inefficiency of the local government. Police protection was almost nonexistent; the wharves, streets and highways, they insisted, must "be commodious for business and kept in good repair." The only solution, they agreed, was to obtain control of the situation by petitioning the Legislature for incorporation as a city. One of their allies was Noah Webster, the schoolmaster who spelled his way to fame. But the more numerous farmers could see no benefit to them and objected to dividing Hartford into a city and town.

In December the proponents were encouraged by the separation of East Hartford into a new township, which had the effect of weakening the rural opposition. A committee of 14 was formed to proceed with the petition and to fix the limits of the new city. Retiring Governor Jonathan Trumbull, fully aware of the state's moribund trade, favored not only the Hartford petition, but also those of other towns having ports.

The committee members representing Hartford included Colonel Thomas Seymour, Captain Jonathan Bull, the merchant Peter Colt,

Noah Webster
Watercolor on ivory, 1788.

Noah Webster, and the poet and Hartford Wit John Trumbull. A staunch supporter was Chauncey Goodrich, who would become the city's second mayor and U.S. senator from 1807-1813. At its session in May 1784, the Legislature granted city charters to Hartford as well as to Middletown, New Haven, New London and Norwich. Hartford's boundaries, "beginning at a Place called the Dutch Ground on the Bank of the Great River," covered only the area already settled, which terminated near Washington Street, totaling only 1,700 acres.

On June 18, Thomas Seymour, described as "a smooth and persuasive advocate," was chosen mayor, and a month later the Court of Common Council held its first meeting in the old State and Court House erected in 1719 southeast of the new State House that would be built in 1796. The mayor received no salary, and for 50 years his chief duties were to preside over the Council and to act as judicial magistrate. The four aldermen and 20 councilmen were all leading citizens. The first ordinances enacted were directed at keeping livestock from roaming the muddy streets untended. In 1789 the Legislature granted permission for a lottery to erect new wharves at the foot of State Street.

Mayor Seymour remained in office for 28 years, the longest term in the city's mayoral history. A war veteran, he had risen to second in command of the First Connecticut cavalry regiment. He married Mary Ledyard, sister of Colonel William Ledyard who was slain after surrendering Groton Heights to the British in 1781. Seymour's political career was not confined to being mayor. Elected to the General Assembly in 1774, he represented Hartford in 17 sessions, being speaker of the House five times. In 1793 he began a 10-year term in the Upper House, as the Senate was then called, and also served as chief judge of the Hartford County Court. He resigned as mayor at the age of 77. During the rest of his life he lived in seclusion with his son and died at the age of 94. His grandson, Thomas H. Seymour, became governor of Connecticut in 1850.

Oddly enough, the city of Hartford was not so designated by the politicians until 1859. Until 1896 Hartford continued to operate with two governments—one for the city, the other for the town. The city limits were extended four times and divided into wards. The separation of West Hartford in 1854 reduced the land area to its present size of 18.4 square miles, slightly more than Bridgeport but less than New Haven.

In 1784 the signposts of daily life were the columns of the weekly *Connecticut Courant,* which had started publication 20 years earlier. One could read that the General Assembly passed acts to encourage the destroying of wolves and the growing of raw silk. It also provided for the gradual emancipation of the 6,500 slaves then in the state. There was a $10 reward for a runaway slave and another for the capture of a horse thief ($5 for the horse only). John Caldwell wanted to buy horses for shipment to the West Indies. Hudson & Goodwin, printers of the *Courant,* touted "valuable books" for sale, including the second edition of Webster's *Grammatical Institute.*

ABOVE,
Mary Ledyard (Mrs. Thomas Seymour).
Oil on canvas, 1764.
BELOW,
In 1852 a new seal was designed and approved by the Common Council. It is somewhat like the seal of old Hertford in that it shows a "hart" standing in a "ford." At the base of the shield in which the hart is emblazoned is a fruitful grapevine, symbolizing the state, at the top an American eagle, symbolizing the nation, below is a streamer with the words Post Nubila Phoebus—"After the Clouds, the Sun."

Asa Hopkins advertised drugs and medicines, Joseph Lynde West India rum and wines, while Samuel Pitkin had anchors for sale in his East Hartford store. The schedule for the "stage waggon" to Boston and New Haven was announced. Tickets were available for the newly approved lottery to repair the riverbank at Middletown. Offers of farms and tracts of land in Connecticut and New Hampshire appeared frequently.

Probably the two most exciting events occurred at the end of that decade. Long in favor of a strong central government, Hartford's civic leaders rejoiced when on January 9, 1788, the delegates meeting in the city voted overwhelmingly to ratify the new federal constitution. Connecticut was the first state to do so. The following year President Washington made a ceremonial tour through New England, arriving in Hartford in October, where he was greeted by the Governor's Horse Guard and spent the night at Bull's Tavern. Washington wrote in his diary that he was surprised the city still had no Episcopal Church, but three years later Christ Church, despite bitter opposition from the Congregationalists, was erected.

Without doubt the most influential person in Hartford at this time was Jeremiah Wadsworth, the city's wealthiest merchant. During the Revolution he had managed to mix profit with patriotism. He was not only Washington's commissary general of purchases, but also had the responsibility for supplying the French allied forces. Returning from Europe after collecting the gold owed him by the French government, he spearheaded Hartford's return to prosperity. He served as an alder-

TOP,
Thomas Y. Seymour.
Silhouette, c. 1811.
MIDDLE,
Chauncey Goodrich.
Pastel, c. 1814.
BOTTOM,
Jonathan Brace, Jr.
Engraving, c. 1800.
RIGHT,
Colonel Jeremiah Halsey.
Oil on canvas, c. 1796.
Earliest known view of Old State
House appears in background of
this portrait.

man or councilman until his death and as a congressman from 1789–1795.

In 1788 he was the principal organizer of the Hartford Woolen Manufactory, the first mill of its kind in the United States. A speculative venture, the mill on the Little River in what is now Bushnell Park was a desperate effort to compete with British imports. Although the Legislature granted the stockholders permission to conduct a lottery for the purpose of buying new equipment, "this precious embryo," as Alexander Hamilton called it, survived only seven and a half years. It lacked an adequate market, and its broadcloth—although worn by President Washington at his first inauguration in 1789—was inferior in quality to English goods. Nevertheless, the Hartford Woolen Manufactory was an important milestone in anticipating the transformation, some 25 years later, of merchant capitalists like Wadsworth into industrialists.

Besides pioneering in manufacturing, Wadsworth promoted Hartford's first banking institution and engaged in an insurance partnership, both of which were harbingers of the city's future preeminence as a financial center.

This remarkable man was also one of the chief backers of a new State House, contributing the first and largest subscription to the building fund—all of $500. The inadequacy of the old wooden capitol was apparent by 1792, and Charles Bulfinch of Boston was retained to design the new structure. Initially, it was proposed to finance it through private donations with matching funds from the state. More than $3,600 was raised from 51 contributors; $5,000 more came from the city and county. Even after adding the state's match, the total fell far short of the amount needed. The committee in charge, men like John Chester, Noadiah Hooker, John Caldwell, John Trumbull and John Morgan, appealed to the General Assembly in May 1793, for permission to conduct a lottery. There were to be 26,667 tickets offered at $5 each, of which about one-third would share in prizes ranging from $10 to $8,000. If all the tickets were sold, the managers would realize $16,667.

The drawing for the winners was promised to take place when three-fourths of the tickets had been purchased, but the goal was not reached for two years, despite a desperate effort to boost sales by offering insurance guaranteeing a prize! The managers blamed in part the lack of a "Spirit of Enterprise in Lottery speculations" on the dearth of money "which has been occasioned by the unreasonable Spoliations & Detention of American property by foreign nations." Without doubt the fortunes of Hartford merchants and shipowners were being severely affected by the attempts of the French and English to throttle America's maritime trade. Finally, the new State House was finished in 1796 at a cost of $52,480. The old building, in true Yankee fashion, was moved over to Church Street and converted into a rooming house.

In a sense, Wadsworth's death in 1804 marked the end of the Revolutionary era in Hartford. He was mourned by the *Courant* as the city's "greatest benefactor" and by his close friend David Humphreys as "always the protector and guardian of the widow, the fatherless and the distressed."

Early in the 19th century three momentous events severely shook the customary serenity of Connecticut. First, the War of 1812 that crippled shipping and trade; second, the Hartford Convention in 1814 at the State House to protest that unpopular war; and third, the state's first constitutional convention, also held at the State House, in 1818.

Hartford State-House LOTTERY.

THE Managers of the Lottery granted by the Legiſlature of this State, towards building a STATE-HOUSE in HARTFORD, preſent to the Public the following

SCHEME.

1	Prize of	8000 Dollars is	8000
1		4000	4000
1		2000	2000
2		1000	2000
8		500	4000
26		200	5200
50		100	5000
100		50	5000
100		40	4000
200		30	6000
400		20	8000
8000		10	80000
1	laſt drawn Blank		135
8890	Prizes.		133,335
17777	Blanks.		
26667	Tickets at 5 Dollars each,	is	133,335

NOT TWO BLANKS TO A PRIZE.

Subject to a Deduction of Twelve and an Half per Cent.

THE drawing of the Lottery ſhall commence as ſoon as Three Fourths of the Tickets are Sold. A Liſt of the Fortunate Numbers ſhall be immediately printed in Meſſ'rs HUDSON & GOODWIN's Paper at Hartford, and forwarded to all the Agents out of this State, who may diſpoſe of Tickets. Thoſe prizes not demanded in ſix months after the drawing ſhall be completed, will be conſidered as generouſly given for the benefit of the Lottery.

JOHN CHESTER,
NOADIAH HOOKER,
JOHN CALDWELL, } Managers.
JOHN TRUMBULL,
JOHN MORGAN,

Hartford, June 1793.

The Hartford Convention brought together 26 representatives from the New England states to discuss their common grievances. Most were staunch Federalists, sharply critical of the radical and, to them, ruinous policies of President James Madison. The secret meeting resulted in a very bad press. The delegates were accused of "sowing the seeds of dissension and disunion." Because peace was declared within the next few months, the decisions reached came to naught.

Four years later the Constitutional Convention faced up to the new economic and social conditions in the state. The old Federalist party, unable to cope with the complex problems spawned after the Revolution, had gradually declined in power. The younger generation, through the Republican-Tolerationist party, insisted that Connecticut needed an up-to-date constitution to replace the old Royal Charter procured from King Charles II of England in 1662. The party's leader was Oliver Wolcott Jr., son and grandson of former governors, who the next year would be elected governor himself.

The chief bone of contention was the great power vested in the Congregational Church, which since Colonial days had been tax-supported as the official religion of Connecticut. Growing numbers of Episcopalians and other Protestant denominations objected fiercely to being forced to contribute to this old bastion of the Puritan hierarchy. The Constitutional Convention of 1818 actually brought about a bloodless revolution by disestablishing the Congregational Church and allowing other Christian churches to flourish. Jews were not granted this privilege until 1842. Many new laws were passed that enabled the state to deal more realistically with the challenge of a changing economy and a population that included more and more people of different ethnic and religious backgrounds.

For three and a half centuries numerous Hartfordians like Wadsworth have distinguished themselves not only in business but also by participation in the democratic process as mayors, legislators, congressmen and congresswomen, senators and governors. Eighteen became governor, including the first five governors of the colony who served from 1639 to 1658. In addition, 10 U.S. senators and 29 congressmen elected between 1789 and 1984 have called Hartford their home.

Since the city's incorporation in 1784, there have been 57 mayors appointed or elected. Until 1825 mayors were chosen by the General Assembly. Seymour's term of 28 years was the longest of all. Like the six who followed him, he was a graduate of Yale and a lawyer by profession. In fact, more than 40 percent of all Hartford's mayors were trained in the law, and 15 have attended Yale College.

In their politics, Hartford's mayors have been split almost evenly between Democrats and Republicans, 25 to 22, with the rest Federalists, Whigs or Independents. One mayor went on to become governor and another served two terms in Congress after the Civil War. The first mayor to be elected by popular vote, Nathaniel Terry (1824-1831), was not only president of the Hartford Bank (now Connecticut National Bank) but also the leading incorporator of the Hartford Fire Insurance Company and its first president.

For most of the 19th century, politics were controlled by the Protestant elite and unfortunately corrupted by the rise of anti-Catholic sentiment. Preachers like Horace Bushnell, who equated Protestantism with Republicanism, felt that immigration would destroy the American heritage and saw the Irish as crowding the "alms-houses, the prisons and the potters' fields." Along with the educator Henry Barnard, Bushnell

Oliver Wolcott, Jr.
Oil on canvas, c. 1820.

13

John M. Niles.
Ambrotype, c. 1856.

lobbied for a state-supported public school system as the best way of absorbing the foreign-born into the Anglo-Saxon culture through a Protestant-based curriculum. The Catholics responded by establishing their own schools, and by 1854 nearly 700 Catholic boys were attending St. Patrick's free school and two others in Hartford.

Champion of the nativist viewpoint was the *Hartford Courant* and its bigoted editor Theodore Dwight, brother of Timothy Dwight, president of Yale. The *Courant* referred to the Irish section of Hartford as "Pigville," accused Catholics of wanting to eliminate the Protestant Bible from public schools and feared the competition of their growing numbers against the native-born for lower-skilled jobs. But immigrants had a staunch defender in the person of John M. Niles, who founded the *Hartford Times* and at once became the other paper's severest critic. Under Niles' leadership, the Democrats in Connecticut nearly tripled their membership, and in 1833 succeeded in electing Henry W. Edwards of New Haven governor.

Like Bridgeport and New Haven, Hartford doubled in size between 1820 and 1850, but in the latter year only one in five of its 17,750 residents was not native-born. A major change came about, the adoption of ward-based representation, that considerably bolstered the power of Irish voters. Prior to that time all the seats on the City Council were filled in annual at-large elections, in which the most prominent men were invariably elected. To placate the opposition, the Whigs allotted about one-third of the seats to Democrats. But in 1850 a Democratic Legislature approved a charter revision doing away with the at-large system, and instead provided for the election of an alderman and four councilmen from each of the six wards.

In the election of 1851 the only ward that went Democratic, the Sixth, coincided with the principal Irish section of the city, a densely populated area of tenements and small shops. The following year the Sixth Ward succeeded in placing one of its own, James Mulligan, a foundry worker, on the Council. With the help of Irish voters the Democrats captured the mayoralty in both 1853 and 1854. (But not until 1902 were the Irish able to choose an Irish mayor, Ignatius Sullivan, president of the Central Labor Union, who had the year before achieved prominence in settling Hartford's first city-wide strike.)

By then religious prejudice was the hottest issue in Connecticut politics. With the formation of the notorious Know-Nothing party in 1853 the stage was set for two years of bitter invective and the election of a Know-Nothing governor in 1854, who in his inaugural address questioned the fitness of immigrants to become citizens. As the mouthpiece of Waspism, the *Courant* favored the idea of a 21-year residency requirement to qualify for citizenship, while the *Times,* as the protector of minority rights, argued for assimilation.

In 1856 and 1857 the Know-Nothings won the state election again, although most of the foreign-born in Hartford voted overwhelmingly for the Democrats. But as the issue of slavery rose to a climax, the Know-Nothing influence waned fast. Public opinion was already changing in favor of the Irish immigrants as they became increasingly essential for domestic service, heavy labor and factory jobs.

A young rebel lawyer named Joseph R. Hawley had much to do with creating a new political party in Hartford. In his office in February 1856, before the formation of any national organization, gathered a group of prominent men to organize the Connecticut Republicans.

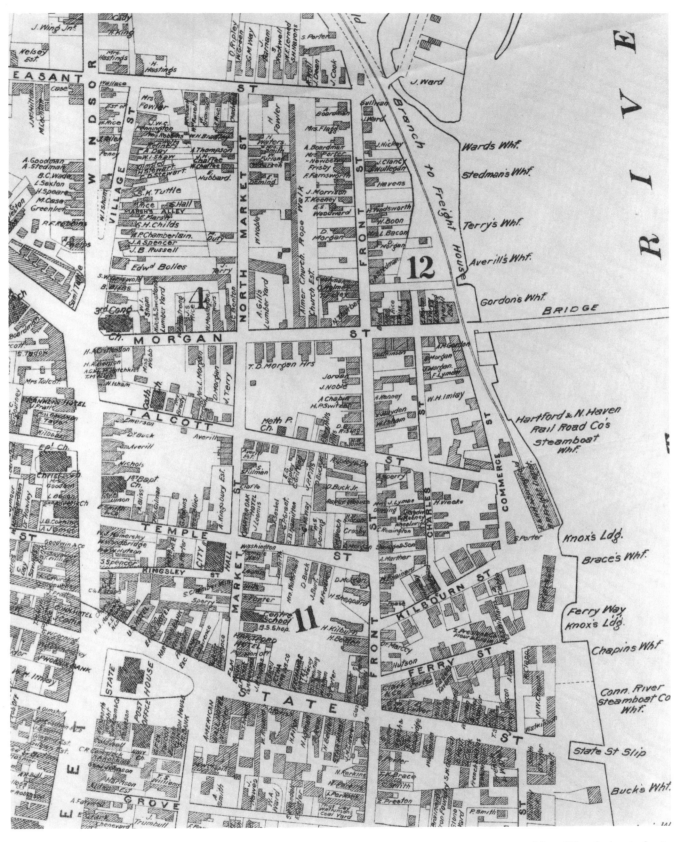

Map of Hartford waterfront,
1850. Detail from the 1902
Municipal Register.

That fall Hawley spearheaded the Fremont campaign to a state-wide victory. He started publication of the *Hartford Evening Press* to promulgate the Republican cause. In 1867 the *Press* would merge with the *Courant,* with Hawley and Charles Dudley Warner as part-owners. Not only was Hawley a Civil War hero, in fact the first man to volunteer in Hartford, he later served as governor for one year, as president of the U.S. Centennial Commission in Philadelphia, as congressman for three terms and as U.S. senator from 1881 until his death in 1905.

No sooner had the Civil War ended than Hartford businessmen plunged into a frenzied period of money-making and business expansion. Nearly 40,000 people lived in the city, half of whom were employed in the several hundred factories. Despite the smokestacks and streets filled with carriages and horse cars, the appearance of the city had improved. The opening of Bushnell Park in 1868 did away with the tanneries and hovels surrounding the Park River. On his first visit to Hartford that year, Mark Twain's impression was, on the whole, favorable, although to his disgust he observed that nobody smoked in the streets and cigar stores were few and far between. He wrote: "I think this is the best built and handsomest town I have ever seen. They call New England the land of steady habits, and I can see the evidence about me that it was not named amiss . . . This is the centre of Connecticut wealth." Indeed, Hartford at that time enjoyed the highest per capita wealth in America, but the great novelist overlooked the existence of the 144 downtown saloons.

Hartford's power structure was dominated by such giants as James G. Batterson, president of the Travelers Insurance Company; the Rev. Francis Goodwin, who did well in real estate and served well by masterminding Hartford's park system; Senator Joseph Hawley, owner of the *Courant;* and Morgan G. Bulkeley. In 1879 the latter became head of Ætna Life; the following year he was elected mayor and for the rest of his life remained as heavily involved in politics as in insurance, becoming a governor of Connecticut (1889–1893) and later succeeding Hawley as U.S. senator (1905–1911).

Women, however, continued to remain second-class citizens for another half century, even though a few liberated ladies struggled to gain equality. In 1869 Frances Ellen Burr joined with Isabella Hooker in calling a convention that marked the founding of the Connecticut Woman Suffrage Association. Lawyer John Hooker, Isabella's husband, prepared various resolutions stressing that political rights for women "would bring to the aid of virtuous men a new and powerful element of good which cannot be spared, and for which there can be no substitute." The two-day convention at Roberts Opera House was packed with Hartford's best people to hear such luminaries as Julia Ward Howe, Henry Ward Beecher, Susan B. Anthony, Elizabeth Cady Stanton and William Lloyd Garrison. Mrs. Hooker and her followers never expected suffrage to blossom out all at once. As Miss Burr philosophized: "One bobolink doesn't make a summer, nor one snowstorm a winter."

Their first success came in 1877 when they persuaded their friend, Governor Richard Hubbard, to champion a law giving married women the same property rights as men. From then on to 1920 it was an uphill and unrewarding battle against the prevailing ideal of womanhood . . . "a beguiling creature, half angel and half idiot." In fact, women were classified legally with "children, idiots and criminals" and thus unworthy of the franchise. Otherwise liberal preachers like Horace Bushnell

ABOVE,
Mayor Ignatius A. Sullivan.
FAR RIGHT,
Senator Joseph R. Hawley.

Woman Suffrage parade,
c. 1915.

regarded woman suffrage as "a reform against nature. . ."

To crown its stature as the leading city of the state, Hartford sought to become the sole capital. Since 1701 legislative sessions had been held alternately in Hartford and New Haven. In a hard fought contest with its sister city, Hartford seized the initiative by offering the state $500,000 toward the erection of a new capitol, and in March 1872 purchased the campus of Trinity College for $600,000. At that time the college was located on the hill that rose between Bushnell Park and Washington Street. The following year Connecticut's voters approved a constitutional amendment making Hartford the permanent seat of state government.

The construction of the new capitol proved to be one of the worst boondoggles in the state's history. From the time the first building commission was appointed, it took eight years (1871 to 1879) before a regular session of the Legislature could assemble in its new quarters, while in the fall of that year City Hall moved into the vacated Old State House. Charged with holding the cost to $1 million, the members were unable to agree on any of the first five designs submitted. In May of 1873 they resigned, by which time the foundations had been laid, and the Legislature ordered all work stopped until newly-elected Governor Charles R. Ingersoll, a Democrat, could appoint another commission.

He chose as chairman Alfred E. Burr, the liberal publisher of the *Times* and chief proponent of having the city purchase the land from Trinity College. Also on the commission was General William Franklin, vice-president of Colt's Patent Firearms Company, who played a key role because of his engineering background. They found themselves in a hornet's nest of wrangling over esthetics and specifications. Burr himself strongly objected to having a Tuscan clock tower instead of the traditional New England Bulfinch dome. The new commission insisted on Gothic architecture, even though no other state capitol had been built in this style and, from 11 more plans, finally selected Richard Upjohn's "Gothic Revival" design.

James G. Batterson, who still ran his stone works as well as the fledgling Travelers Insurance Company, won the building contract with a bid of $875,000. Unfortunately, the original masonry work was faulty; when half completed, the dome tower collapsed into a pile of rubble. Other construction difficulties followed, so that by the time the East Canaan marble, the gilded dome, the statuary, the portraits, the library on the third floor, and the furnishings of 80 rooms were all in place, the cost had escalated to three times the original authorization. Nonetheless, the public reaction to the opulent structure was ecstatic. Over the years the state's unique capitol has been the subject of architectural ridicule and legislative distress because of its dysfunctional layout, but refurbished after its first century, the people of Hartford have grown accustomed to its face.

The 1870s ended in a spectacular blaze of light. On September 17, the anniversary of the Battle of Antietam, thousands of Civil War veterans and their followers gathered in Hartford for an impressive parade, patriotic speeches and a sumptuous dinner under tents pitched in Bushnell Park. During the parade the entire city turned out to watch the battle flags carried from the Hartford Arsenal to the Capitol for placement in permanent cases. When darkness fell, the sky lit up magically, not with torches or gas jets, but with arc lights. It was as dramatic and as trailblazing an event as had ever been seen in Hartford.

State Capitol, c. 1878.

On top of the Capitol dome and around Bushnell Park powerful lamps, powered by a small Baxter steam engine borrowed from the Colt factory, had been strategically placed. A 3,000 candlepower searchlight, with colored lenses, played at random about the park from the roof of the Plimpton building on Jewell Street. For three hours the amazed spectators, some 30,000, marveled at the display.

The idea for the illumination came from the fertile brain of Mayor Bulkeley. Determined that an independent electric utility could best serve the city, he next persuaded the Legislature to pass a bill incorporating the Hartford Electric Light Company. A.C. Dunham became president, and in April 1883, the first 21 electric lights were turned on at the railroad station and along Main and Asylum streets. In rapid succession lights were installed in Brown Thomson's "One Price Clothing Store," Heublein's Saloon and two other stores; before the end of the first month four dynamos were humming and 100 lights made clear that the age of electricity had arrived.

In the first half of this century Hartford's political leadership was divided fairly evenly between the Republican old guard and Irish Democrats, with the latter gradually getting the upper hand. Unlike other cities, Hartford's politics, though raucous in nature and replete with patronage, were seldom marred by serious scandal. It is true that during Prohibition Mayor Walter E. Batterson did little to interfere with the illegal operation of the 178 saloons that had become speakeasies. And after its repeal no one could get a liquor license unless he agreed to sell Boss Tony Zazzaro's Dover Ale. These were the days when J. Henry

RIGHT,
Dedication of the Civil War Memorial Arch in 1886. Designed by Hartford Architect George Keller. During the Civil War more than 4,000 soldiers and sailors from the city bore arms, of whom 400 died.

John M. Bailey.

Roraback of Prospect Avenue ran the state Republican machine with an iron hand, and Mayor Thomas J. Spellacy used the political muscle of the Democrats to build the Hartford dike after the devastating floods of 1936 and 1938. It was Spellacy who launched the brilliant political career of John M. Bailey, Connecticut's Democratic chairman from 1946 until his death in 1975.

But partisan politics of the rough and tumble kind disappeared for a while in the late 1940s when the Republicans captured the mayoralty and joined forces with a reform group called the Citizens Charter Committee. Out went the shabby ward and aldermanic system; in came the more efficient but less colorful council-manager form of government, with the office of mayor reduced to ceremonial status. The Democrats, however, could not long abide the blandness of nonpartisanship. Today, outnumbering the Republicans seven-to-one, they battle among themselves for the six of the nine Council seats that their dominance guarantees them in biennial elections.

In the 1960s Hartford's power structure, spearheaded by the Greater Hartford Chamber of Commerce, made a determined effort to establish regional government to solve the city's economic problems. An organization called Hartford Process was created and funded to create a new town in eastern Connecticut, to which the business leaders hoped they could attract Hartford's poorer residents. However, the suburbs, traditionally protective of their autonomy, shunned regionalism in any form, and Hartford voters objected because they feared their political power would be diluted by the more numerous suburban vote.

Other than those mentioned, the mayors with outstanding records have all held office since 1920:

Newton C. Brainard (1920–1922) Brainard was responsible for the city's airport, which was named after him, and as chairman of the Fine Arts Commission rescued the Old State House from demolition and contributed some of its furnishings. He was also a prominent businessman and philanthropist.

Thomas J. Spellacy (1935–1943) For 50 years a political gladiator and Democratic power broker, Spellacy first ran for mayor in 1911 against Louis R. Cheney (1912-1914) and lost. After World War I, he served as U.S. assistant attorney general and in 1922 was defeated in a Senate race by George P. McLean of Simsbury. Appointed mayor in 1935 after the death of John Pilgard, he was thrice re-elected. His administration coped with three emergencies, the Flood of 1936, the Hurricane of 1938 and the start of World War II. He formed Hartford's Flood Commission and Housing Authority.

William H. Mortensen (1943–1945) One of the last of the city's "strong mayors," Mortensen, a Republican, lowered the tax rate. For 40 years he was managing director of the Bushnell Memorial Hall. Against bitter opposition from both political parties, but with the backing of "Long Tom" Spellacy, Mortensen organized the Citizens Charter Commission to establish a council-manager form of local government, which was approved by the voters in December 1946.

Edward N. Allen (1946–1948) A large, friendly man, "Ned" Allen enjoyed Republican politics, even though he was president of Sage-Allen, the department store. He went on to become lieutenant gover-

Antonina P. Uccello

nor (1951-1955). His wife Mildred served as secretary of the state from 1955-1959.

Cyril Coleman (1948–1951) Succeeded Republican Edward N. Allen as the first of the "weak mayors" under the new charter, which designated the candidate receiving the highest number of votes as the titular head of the city. Although a Democrat, Coleman strongly believed in nonpartisan elections.

Joseph V. Cronin (1951–1953, 1955–1957) Served on the Charter Commission and was elected to the first council in 1947. He was the second labor leader to be chosen mayor.

Dominick J. Delucco (1953–1955) The first Italian-American to become mayor. Quitting school at age 14, he worked his way up from laborer and truck driver to restaurant owner. Warm-hearted, with a great love for the city, he was the hero of the man on the street.

Antonina P. Uccello (1967–1971) The last Republican mayor, Ann was also the first woman mayor of Hartford, an honor she claimed was made possible by the council-manager system.

George A. Athanson (1971–1981) Born in the Frog Hollow area, the son of Greek immigrants, Athanson stayed in office for 10 years, second in duration only to Thomas Seymour's 28 years.

Thirman L. Milner (1981–   ) Born in Hartford in 1933, a third generation native, Milner grew up in the North End, served in the Air Force, and was a state representative from 1979–1981. He was the first black to be elected mayor in any New England city.

RIGHT,
Mayor Thomas J. Spellacy.

Mayors Of the City of Hartford

1784–1812	Thomas Seymour[1] F		1902–1904	Ignatius A. Sullivan D
1812–1815	Chauncey Goodrich F		1904–1908	William F. Henney R
1815–1824	Jonathan Brace F		1908–1910	Edward W. Hooker R
1824–1831	Nathaniel Terry W		1910–1912	Edward L. Smith D
1831–1835	Thomas S. Williams W		1912–1914	Louis R. Cheney R
1835–1835	Henry L. Ellsworth[2] D		1914–1916	Joseph H. Lawler D
1835–1835	Jared Griswold[3] W		1916–1918	Frank A. Hagarty R
1835–1836	Jeremy Hoadley W		1918–1920	Richard J. Kinsella D
1836–1840	Henry Hudson W		1920–1922	Newton C. Brainard R
1840–1843	Thomas K. Brace[2] W		1922–1924	Richard J. Kinsella D
1843–1847	Amos M. Collins D		1924–1928	Norman C. Stevens R
1847–1851	Philip Ripley D		1928–1931	Walter E. Batterson R
1851–1853	Ebenezer Flower D		1931–1933	William J. Rankin D
1853–1854	William J. Hamersley D		1933–1935	Joseph W. Beach R
1854–1858	Henry C. Deming D		1935–1935	John A. Pilgard[3] D
1858–1860	Timothy M. Allyn R		1935–1943	Thomas J. Spellacy D
1860–1862	Henry C. Deming D		1943–1943	Dennis P. O'Connor D
1862–1862	Charles Benton D		1943–1945	William H. Mortensen R
1862–1864	William J. Hamersley D		1945–1946	Cornelius A. Moylan R
1864–1866	Allyn S. Stillman R		1946–1948	Edward N. Allen R
1866–1872	Charles R. Chapman D		1948–1951	Cyril Coleman D
1872–1874	Henry C. Robinson R		1951–1953	Joseph V. Cronin D
1874–1878	Joseph H. Sprague D		1953–1955	Dominick J. DeLucco D
1878–1880	George G. Sumner D		1955–1957	Joseph V. Cronin D
1880–1888	Morgan G. Bulkeley R		1957–1960	James H. Kinsella D
1888–1890	John G. Root R		1960–1961	Dominick J. DeLucco D
1890–1892	Henry C. Dwight R		1961–1965	William E. Glynn D
1892–1894	William Waldo Hyde D		1965–1967	George B. Kinsella D
1894–1896	Leverett Brainard R		1967–1971	Antonina P. Uccello R
1896–1900	Miles B. Preston D		1971–1981	George A. Athanson D
1900–1902	Alexander Harbison R		1981–	Thirman L. Milner D

[1] Resigned to the General Assembly
[2] Resigned
[3] Died before taking oath of office
[4] Died in office

D Democrat
F Federalist
R Republican
W Whig

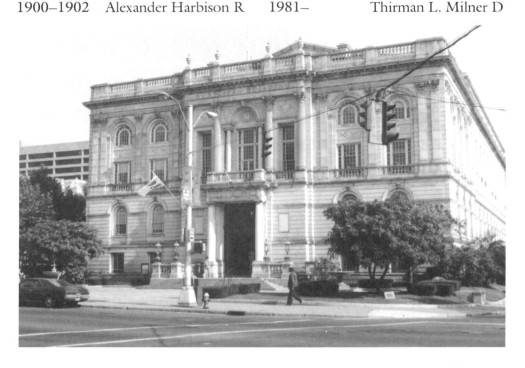

Municipal Building.

View of The City of Hartford.
Hand-colored aquatint, 1841.

The Connecticut River Valley, especially the 70 miles from Enfield to Long Island, can be viewed as a microcosm of American social development in a river-oriented environment—the steady but slow growth of river towns constrained to some extent by natural conditions and altered mainly by changing forms of transportation.

Until the 1840s Hartford was known as the Port of Hartford because of its location on the Connecticut River. The river provided Hartford's merchants, manufacturers and nearby farmers with a vital means of transportation that enabled them to trade with other river and sea ports in this country, the West Indies, Europe, Africa and, eventually, the Pacific Islands and Asia. The voyage from the river's mouth at Saybrook up to Hartford commonly took two weeks, almost as much time as that needed to sail all the way from the Caribbean to the Connecticut coast! For this reason, and because the river was at best shallow, many Hartford captains also dispatched larger vessels from New London's fine, deep harbor.

Even so, Hartford's affluent merchants and sea captains were known to other Yankee traders and skippers who lived in the downstream towns that bordered the Connecticut as the "River Gods" because Hartford was the farthest upstream port accessible to comparatively deep-draft sailing vessels . . . sloops, schooners and brigs. These sturdily constructed craft were popularly known as "horse jockeys" because they carried many horses and mules down to the Caribbean. Cargos also included lumber, barrel staves, coarse cloth, hardware, dried local fish, live poultry, pearl and pot ash, salt pork, tobacco, onions and dried corn. Connecticut kiln-dried cornmeal became so abundant that it was almost a drug on the market. West Indian planters imported great quantities of this meal to feed their numerous slaves.

More than 36 of the city's leading merchants had warehouses down by the docks where they stored their imports from the Indies. Imports included rum, sugar, molasses, coffee and spices. In fact, more West Indian rum was imported into Connecticut in proportion to the state's total trade than into any other state in the Union! "Country Rum" was also distilled locally from West Indian molasses. By 1810 more than 500 distilleries in Connecticut, centered chiefly in Hartford County, produced 1,374,000 gallons of spirits annually. The Hartford firm of Ward and Bartholomew, established in 1804, did a large and profitable business in manufacturing rum stills and church bells!

North of the Port of Hartford to the upriver towns in Massachusetts, New Hampshire and Vermont, all goods had to be transported on flatboats capable of traversing the numerous rapids and falls. The Connecticut River is unique in New England in that it flows from lakes in Canada all the way to Long Island Sound, a 400-mile waterway vital to the early prosperity of the entire region because it provided an artery for transportation, trade and travel long before the development of railroads and highways.

A fleet of about 75 flatboats carried this upriver traffic from Hartford. These craft usually had a mast amidships and one or two square sails. Passage was slow, especially when the wind failed to blow. The falls at Enfield were troublesome. Here at least two polemen had to force the boat up against the current, thrusting their long poles hard into the

TOP,
Captain Ashbel Riley of
Wethersfield.
Oil on canvas, 1764.
BOTTOM,
Captain John Barnard of
Hartford.
Painted photograph.

muck and rock of the river bottom. It was rugged work and the men frequently fortified themselves with bracing draughts of West Indian rum.

After disposing of their cargos, flatboats made the comparatively easy voyage back to Hartford loaded with the produce of northern New England, chiefly lumber and brine-soaked beef and pork. Hartford's able shipbuilders thrived because of the superior quality of their materials and workmanship. Logs, floated down in rafts from northern forests, were in great demand as spars, masts and timbers.

Trade from Hartford also went overland. The trails, roads and turnpikes were rough, deeply rutted, and often muddy. However, they were in constant use by people walking, on horseback, in carts and stagecoaches, or in heavy freight wagons that lumbered laboriously from one pothole to the next. The Albany Turnpike, now U.S. 44, was a 100-mile journey.

Some stagecoach companies boasted they could make the trip in just 24 hours. To do this, the horses were kept at a running gait. Passengers, tossed violently from side to side by the lurching of the coach, often complained of seasickness. Some preferred to ride on top of the vehicle, even in bad weather. Brief relief was enjoyed while horses were being changed at the many taverns along the way. Between Hartford and New Hartford alone, in the early 19th century, 21 of these welcome hostelries catered to the needs of man and beast.

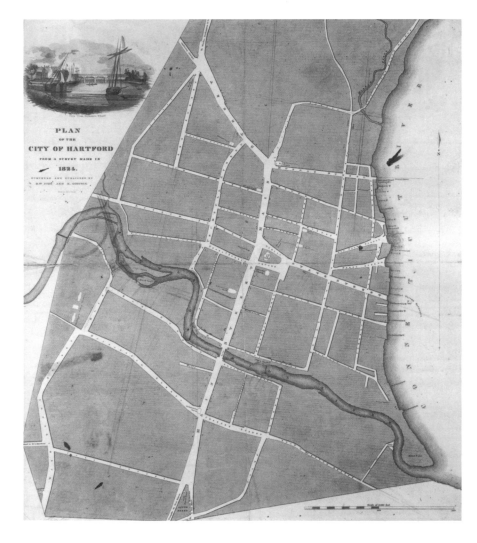

TOP,
A Yankee peddler.
MIDDLE,
Goodwin Tavern on Albany Avenue.
BOTTOM,
Poling a flatboat.
RIGHT,
Plan of The City of Hartford. Engraving, 1824.

Yankee peddlers, their carts filled with Yankee-made goods and imports, also traveled regularly along the roads that constantly reached farther and farther into the interior of the rapidly expanding United States.

In 1815 a new era of power and transportation arrived when the steamboat *Fulton* churned upriver and docked at Hartford for thousands to see. Although Robert Fulton promoted the first successful steamboat, actually John Fitch, a native of Windsor, had used steam for propelling a vessel over water 17 years before Fulton. Another pioneer in steam was Apollos Kinsley of Hartford who drove a steam-propelled vehicle down Main Street in 1797. The *Oliver Ellsworth,* launched in 1824, was the forerunner of a long line of floating palaces that cruised the river in the 19th century, offering regular steamboat services between Hartford, New York and Boston. She was 112 feet long, 24 feet in beam, had an 8-foot draft and a 44-horsepower engine that drove her at a speed of 8 knots.

Travel on early side-wheelers was at best a hazardous undertaking. Once, when the *Oliver Ellsworth* was approaching Old Saybrook lighthouse in the early evening, her boiler exploded, the steam injuring several persons and killing a fireman. She managed to sail into Old Saybrook. Hearing the news, an excited postrider galloped to Hartford, burst in upon the Legislature then sitting in the Old State House and shouted at the wide-eyed lawmakers the memorable words, "The Eliver Olsworth has biled her buster!"

To improve upriver navigation and to demonstrate the Connecticut's superiority for waterborne transportation, Hartford businessmen founded the Connecticut River Banking Company in 1824. Two years later they launched the *Barnet,* a shallow-draft stern-wheeler, which they hoped would replace the old, hand-poled flatboats used to transport goods into Massachusetts, New Hampshire and Vermont. To the amazement of Valley residents the little *Barnet* ascended the river as far as Bellows Falls, Vermont. Its triumphant voyage was greeted by country folk along the way with cheers and the firing of cannon. Encouraged

The "Oliver Ellsworth."
BELOW,
The steamboat "Barnet."

by the steamboat's success, the Bank funded the Connecticut River Company to circumvent the dangerous rapids at Enfield by constructing a six-mile long, 70-foot wide canal. With the help of 400 Irish laborers fresh from the ports of Cork and Galway, the Enfield Canal was opened to traffic in 1829.

Soon stern-wheelers were chugging daily between Hartford and Springfield. In the winter of 1842, one of them carried the English novelist, Charles Dickens, downstream to Hartford where he met the leading representatives of the Standing Order. In his *American Notes* he wrote, "Too much of the old Puritan spirit exists in these parts to the present hour; but its influence has not tended, that I know, to make the people less hard in their bargains, or more equal in their dealings."

Two years after Dickens' voyage, the opening of the railroad between Hartford and Springfield signaled the beginning of the end of the steamboats' short, sweet heyday. At first railroads were bitterly opposed by steamboat, canal, stagecoach and turnpike interests, as well as by landowners. But no one could dispute the fact that puffing, wood-burning steam-engines on wheels radically reduced overland freight costs. Railroad service from New Haven to Hartford had started in 1839. The first locomotives weighed about six tons. Coal replaced wood just before the Civil War, further reducing operating costs. Total railroad mileage jumped from 102 miles in 1840 to 601 in 1860, making the state's concentration of railroads one of the densest in the nation. This was fortunate indeed, because without the ability to send its goods far and wide, Connecticut industry could never have grown as it did.

During the 19th century the old river port of Hartford gradually developed into a major railroad hub and manufacturing center. Immigrants from foreign lands poured into the city to fill the new factory jobs. Between 1820 and 1860 the city's population expanded from 6,901 to 29,150 people. In 1849 a handsome new railroad station, Union Station, was constructed just east of Asylum Hill. At first the railroad tracks crossed Asylum Street at street level. Later, in 1887, the station was radically redesigned to carry trains on a trestle above the street, thus eliminating a major traffic hazard.

In the late 1890s the Pope Manufacturing Company pioneered in making both electric and gasoline powered automobiles . . . a new form of transportation that eventually would reduce the importance of the railroad. The company also understandably became a major promoter of a nation-wide highway system.

Aircraft transportation became a reality when the first airmail was delivered to the city in 1918. At that time the golf course at Goodwin Park was used as a landing field, no other facilities near Hartford being available. A couple of years later two visiting Army airmen were killed trying to land on that golf course, so Hartford's mayor, Newton C. Brainard, determined to build a proper landing field. Named in his honor, Brainard Field . . . now the Hartford-Brainard Airport . . . was dedicated June 12, 1921. It is the second oldest municipal airport in the nation. Charles Lindbergh, on a goodwill tour of the United States after his sensational flight across the Atlantic to Paris, visited Brainard Airport in 1927 where a crowd of 25,000 gathered to greet him.

Today Hartford-Brainard continues to be very busy. It provides excellent facilities for general aviation and light aircraft. Only two miles from the city's business district, Brainard is used by many corporate planes. Charter and taxi services are available. Every evening planes carrying cancelled checks take off from Hartford-Brainard for other American financial centers like New York and Boston. Bradley International Airport at Windsor Locks is the most important airport in the Capitol Region, followed by Hartford-Brainard which is now under the management of the Connecticut Bureau of Aeronautics.

As the Space Age dawned, it became increasingly obvious that efficient communication systems were as important to the prosperity of Hartford as transportation. In 1973 the Southern New England Telephone Company established a sophisticated communications center

TOP RIGHT,
Union Railroad Station, c. 1898.
TOP,
Toll tickets, Hartford & New Haven turnpike. Engraving, c. 1798.
BOTTOM,
Pope-Hartford Touring Car, 1909.

with the capacity of rapidly reaching points all over the earth. Computers, too, are essential to modern, post-industrial Hartford. Because storing, managing and retrieving information is a major activity of banks and insurance companies, and because Hartford's huge, multi-national companies have millions of policies in force world-wide, computers now provide them instantly with all kinds of essential data.

By sea, by land, by air, and now by satellite, Hartford has kept abreast of the latest developments in transportation and communication.

The Riverfront

1614   The Dutch explorer Adriaen Block sailed the first American-built ship, the *Onrust*, up the Connecticut River as far as Enfield Falls.

1633   The Dutch set up a trading post, House of Hope, at the mouth of the Park River.

1636   Thomas Hooker arrived overland to found Hartford—the beginning of the westward movement.

1649   First Connecticut-built ship launched in Wethersfield. Until the end of the 17th century, the sandbars between Wethersfield and Hartford prevented Hartford from becoming a commercial port.

1700   Small shipyards appeared from Saybrook to Windsor; the colony's first industry was building ships, over 4,000 of which were built on the Connecticut River, most of them from 1796 to 1816.

1731   Hartford had only six little ships listed in its inventory.

1764   An English officer visiting the city of Hartford wrote: "Here they build vessels for the lumber trade to the West Indies—from 100 to 150 tons—and float them down in freshes, spring and fall."

1773   Hartford's leading merchant and sea captain, Jeremiah Wadsworth, undertook to improve river navigation by persuading the Legislature to raise money by lottery for marking the Saybrook bar. Even at high tide, sloops and schooners filled with cargo were unable to reach Hartford, and most of them had to unload at Wethersfield.

1790   Hartford's population in the first census totaled 4,100, less than Middletown, only 300 more than Wethersfield.

1800   The Union Company, headed by John Caldwell, president of the Hartford Bank and grandfather of Samuel Colt, and John Morgan, grandfather of J.P. Morgan, obtained a charter to deepen the riverbed below Hartford to build wharves and to collect tolls to pay for these improvements.

Salmon ceased to spawn in the river because of upstream dams.

1810   John Morgan was the biggest shipowner having two brigs, 11 ships and one schooner in foreign trade. Joint underwriting of marine risks in Morgan's coffeehouse led to the beginning of Hartford's insurance industry with the founding of the Hartford Fire Insurance Company in 1810.

1815   The first steamboat, the *Fulton*, churned upriver.

1818   The first Connecticut-built steamboat launched at Hartford to serve as a river tow-boat.

1824   Steamboats ran to New York thrice weekly and the *Oliver Ellsworth*, first in a long line of floating palaces, entered service— 112 feet long, carrying 400 passengers.

1844   River traffic at its peak. In one year alone, Hartford recorded 2,000 arrivals and departures of sail and steam vessels at her 20 wharves. Completion of the railroad to Springfield signaled the end of upriver traffic.

Hartford Yacht Club

1854 The great flood of May 1 isolated the city. Charles H. Dexter of Windsor Locks, remembering that he had a note due at the Hartford Bank, chartered a small steamboat to take him downriver. The captain piloted his vessel right up State Street, moored alongside Bowles Drug Store on Front Street, where Dexter disembarked and discharged his obligation.

1855 Samuel Colt completed his great armory, dock and dike, which stood until the flood of 1936.

Hartford built a reservoir on Lord's Hill (site of the present Hartford Insurance Group) and pumped water from the river.

1866 At the port of Hartford, 600,000 tons were unloaded and over 26,000 passengers arrived or departed. (As late as 1911, almost 700,000 tons of various materials were handled at Hartford.)

1867 The river was so polluted that its water was no longer potable and pumping water to the reservoir ended.

1868 Completion of Bushnell Park shifted the center of the city away from the river.

1884 The chairman of the State Board of Agriculture said: "Hartford sits nervously in the lap of what was once one of the fairest and sweetest and is now one of the filthiest valleys in the world."

1889 The Board of Trade, the predecessor to the Chamber of Commerce, commented in its annual report: "The principal streets of Hartford are for the most part broad, well-paved and lighted by electricity. Its main business and resident parts are from 50 to 100 feet above the Connecticut and Park rivers, which later bisects the town and affords excellent facilities for sewage."

1895 Organization of the Hartford Yacht Club, the third oldest in the country. Annual regattas were held on the Connecticut River.

1914 Hartford voters approved the spending of $500,000 to buy riverfront land for public docks, boat landings, and a promenade, but the project never materialized.

1929 Activity on the Hartford's dock dwindled so much that the arrival of a three-masted, blue-nosed schooner from Nova Scotia with a cargo of lumber caused considerable excitement.

1931 The *Hartford* made its last voyage, ending steamboat service, although coal barges continued to ply the river.

1936 Hartford's worst flood crested at 37 1/2 feet, six feet above the previous record. The Colt dike was demolished and the South Meadows inundated.

1938 New England's first hurricane in over a century wreaked more havoc. As a direct result of these two natural disasters, Hartford's face was changed for good. Hartford's Flood Commission obtained $10 million to build a new 45-foot high dike and a pumping station in Bushnell Park for the Park River.

1939 Fire destroyed the remaining docks.

1941 Construction of the new dike wiped out the entire dock area from Bulkeley Bridge to the Park River and covered the remains of the old Yacht Club. The Park River itself was buried under a conduit over which the Whitehead Highway was built.

1946 Largest vessel ever to navigate the river, LST #722, anchored in Hartford as a training ship for the Naval Reserve.

1950   River commerce was limited to oil barges carrying three million tons a year to tank farms in Wethersfield and East Hartford.

1951   The new highway along the riverfront west of the dike was completed to Windsor.

1964   The *Dolly Madison* offered river cruises, operating from a temporary dock near Wawarme Avenue. The State Health Commissioner said the river had been unfit for swimming for 50 years.

1965   At Riverside Park a boat launching ramp 200 feet wide and a parking lot for 300 cars were completed; Trinity College crews raced on the river.

1967   Connecticut's clean water program was passed by the General Assembly. Millions appropriated for secondary waste treatment facilities like the MDC plant in the South Meadows.

1980   Connecticut River 80 percent cleaner from Massachusetts to the mouth. Salmon begin to return with the installation of fish ladders at Holyoke and upstream and the maturing of stocking programs.

1985   Organized in 1980, Riverfront Recapture, Inc. completed the first phase of a multimillion-dollar plan to make the river accessible again to the people of Greater Hartford. Over a million dollars spent on restoring Riverside Park, constructing a permanent dock near the Colt Armory and improving the East Hartford riverfront. Future projects include a linear park and riverwalk from Wethersfield to Windsor, a pedestrian walkway on Founders Bridge and a large plaza over the highway in the center of Hartford.

Boating on the Connecticut River, c. 1900.

Front Street, April 1906.

Hartford's Streets

The story of old Hartford is eloquently revealed through the names of its streets. As late as 1819 the entire town had only 38 streets, none of them paved. At times the mud on Main Street was so deep that ladies desiring to cross went on horseback to protect their clothing. In 1830 a story was published about a Hartford citizen who saw a hat lying in the road north of the Old State House. Lifting it, he found a man underneath. Asked if help was needed, the man replied, "No thanks, I have a good horse under me and I guess we'll get through!"

From mud, the streets gradually progressed to loose gravel, then to water-bound and oil-bound macadam, followed by concrete and asphalt surfaces around 1895. Until 1920 abutting owners paid for a portion of the cost of street improvements. From 1792 to 1872 six chartered turnpike companies controlled the main arteries in and out of Hartford—Albany Avenue to Albany; Farmington Avenue to Farmington and Litchfield; Blue Hills Avenue to Granby; Maple Avenue to New Haven; Park Street to Bristol; and Wethersfield Avenue to Middletown.

Main Street, originally known as King's Highway, has seen many historical moments. During the Revolution Generals Washington and Knox, Alexander Hamilton and Lafayette strode up Main Street to greet Rochambeau and his French officers in Central Row, after which they rode to Wethersfield to plan the campaign that ended in victory at Yorktown. Over the centuries, up and down Main, have paraded soldiers and civilians celebrating victories and anniversaries, promoting causes like War Bonds and Woman's Suffrage, escorting celebrities like President Taft and Charles Lindbergh, or heralding the arrival of the Barnum & Bailey Circus.

Thomas Hooker Square marks the location of the first meeting house erected by Hartford's founder. Here he preached his famous sermon in 1638 that sowed the seed of representative government in America, saying: "The foundation of authority is laid firstly in the free consent of the people." Likewise, Constitution Plaza (although not a street) commemorates the adoption of the Fundamental Orders of 1639, the first written constitution in the world, inspired by Hooker's sermon. The Old State House, the Atheneum, Center Congregational Church, the Ancient Burying Ground, and the McCook homestead, all on Main Street, are cherished landmarks that fortunately have not perished in the name of progress.

In the 1630s, Prospect Street was called Meetinghouse Alley because it led to the church from the homes of the first pastors, Thomas Hooker and Samuel Stone, (located on the present site of the *Times* building). An early account noted that Hooker also "had a path from his home to the clean and beautiful river that flowed at the foot of the place." The reference was to the Park or Hog River, which later became a public sewer and eventually was buried under the Whitehead Highway.

Charter Oak Avenue, formerly the Ancient Highway, and Charter Oak Place commemorate the famous oak tree in which the colony's Royal Charter was hidden from a rapacious royal governor in 1687. The tree, so enormous that 21 persons could seek protection under it from the elements, fell in August of 1856.

In the vicinity of the Colt Armory the streets carry Dutch and In-

Parade for Charles Lindbergh, July 20, 1927.

dian names, all of them selected by Colonel Samuel Colt in the 1850s. Hendrixsen Avenue refers to the lieutenant accompanying Adriaen Block on the *Onrust*, the first vessel to sail up the Connecticut River to the future site of Hartford, in 1614. Sequassen and Wawarme memorialize, respectively, the sachem of the Suckiaug Indians who conveyed the first land to the English settlers in Hartford in 1636 and the signer of the second deed in 1671, who was sister to the sachem. Huyshope means "House of Hope," after the Dutch trading post at the mouth of the Park River.

There has always been confusion about the Whitehead and Conland "highways," really the approaches to I-91 from Hudson Street. Built over the Park River conduit in 1945, one part is named after Ulmont I. Whitehead Jr., Hartford's first casualty in World War II at Pearl Harbor, and the second after Henry H. Conland, former publisher of the *Hartford Courant* and head of the Bridge Commission.

Asylum Street puzzles every newcomer. It was called the Litchfield Turnpike until the founding of the Connecticut Asylum for the Education and Instruction of the Deaf and Dumb in 1817, which stood on the site of the Hartford Insurance Group for a hundred years.

Columbus Boulevard was opened in 1962 in conjunction with East Side redevelopment. It originally served as the Ancient Highway from the Park River to the North Meadows, but Hartford remembers it best as Front Street, the colorful neighborhood of "Little Italy," whose existence is recognized in the present name.

Governor Street was so named in 1851 after the five governors who at one time or another lived there—Edward Hopkins, George Wyllys, Thomas Welles, and John Webster—all in the 17th century—and Thomas H. Seymour in the middle of the 19th century.

Washington Street was not, as many believe, named after the founder of our country. It took its name instead from Washington College, founded in 1823, now Trinity College, which originally stood on the site of the present Capitol.

Forest and Woodland streets were Hartford's western frontier late into the 19th century. Forest Street was named for Francis Gillette's grove of trees where the Nook Farm literary group settled after 1869. Professor Henry Camp, who built the first house in the woods north of Forest Street, is thought to have named Woodland Street.

Here is the origin of other downtown streets:

Albany Avenue—the stage road to Albany; laid out as Talcott Mountain Turnpike in 1678.

Allyn Street—named after Mayor Timothy M. Allyn.

Ann Street—named after Ann S. Goodwin in 1814 by her sons James and Nathaniel.

Broad Street—named in 1853 because of its width from Farmington Avenue to the railroad tracks.

Capitol Avenue—originally Oil Mill Lane, Rifle Avenue, then College Street from 1827–1874 because Washington College (now Trinity) was located where the Capitol stands.

Church Street—named after Christ Church; opened by Oliver Ellsworth about 1794.

Elm Street—named after the elms that formerly graced Bushnell Park.

Fishfry Street—named after the fishfries that were once popular in the North Meadows during the spring run of alewives.

Capitol Avenue.

Flower Street—named after Ebenezer Flower, mayor of Hartford, 1851–1853.

Gold Street—formerly Factory Lane, its name was changed to Gold in 1846 on account of a gold-beating firm located there.

Grove Street—named for a large grove that stood near the river, where public celebrations were held prior to 1850.

Homestead Avenue—named by Homestead Park Corporation, which opened up the large tract of land in this area for development in 1900.

Market Street—named for the Town Market in 1829.

Park Street—named after Barnard Park in the South End, in 1821 the only park in the city.

Pratt Street—named after John Pratt, through whose farm it was opened in 1814.

Retreat Avenue—named after the Hartford Retreat for the Insane, now the Institute of Living, founded in 1822.

Talcott Street—named after Governor Joseph Talcott in 1761.

The face of Hartford and its streets have radically changed as the result of the gigantic redevelopment and restoration efforts in the downtown area. The first post-war project, Constitution Plaza, in 1962, wiped out several old streets that for generations supported ethinic neighborhoods—especially for the Irish, Italians and Jews. Charles Street, for example, has totally disappeared.

Trumbull Street was widened to give more prominence to the Civic Center and the Sheraton Hotel. Many of the old factories at the lower end of Charter Oak Avenue have been converted into offices. Rundown sections of the city, like Buckingham Street, Congress Street, Charter Oak Place, and Wethersfield Avenue are being resurrected for middle-class housing, their homes restored to their original architectural splendor under the stimulus of preservationists like the Hartford Architecture Conservancy. But most dramatic are the new "skyscrapers" that have risen to fill the expanding need for modern office space for insurance and other service-oriented companies. One of them—CityPlace—is taller than the Travelers Tower, which since 1919 had been Hartford's highest landmark.

Main Street Looking South c. 1868.

ÆTNA INSURANCE COMPANY

Vignette from a circular.
Engraving, 1828.

The Rise of Banking and Insurance

Hartford's preeminence as a financial center second in importance only to Boston and New York rests on the solid foundation of two basic commercial ideas that derived from the Puritan heritage of its capitalists during the late 18th and early 19th centuries. These were: sound credit and calculated risk.

Even the first settlers shared a double-barreled vision of the good life. On the one hand they were concerned with spiritual salvation; on the other, they appreciated the need to survive and prosper. In fact, worldly success was often viewed as a sign of being "elected" to saint-hood. The basis of the famous Puritan work ethic was the conviction that godliness must be demonstrated by usefulness. The famous 17th century Puritan divine, Cotton Mather, said every Christian had two callings, first to serve the Lord and then "a personal calling, or a particular employment, by which his usefulness, in his neighborhood, is distinguished . . . this that he may glorify God, by the doing of good for others, and the getting of good for himself."

This credo amounted to practical idealism. A Congregationalist was a person with his head in the clouds but his feet on the ground. He did not countenance aggrandizement or exploitation. To the contrary, ostentatious display of wealth was deplored, and the obligation to care for the "deserving poor" was mandatory. For the most part, Hartford citizens were neither very rich nor very poor. Instead, they aspired to become a sober and sound middle class.

Nowhere was this credo better demonstrated than in banking and insurance. They both evolved out of the city's functioning as a busy river port and its dependence to a large extent on maritime trade with the West Indies and coastal cities. Captains and merchants used to gather down by the wharves on the Connecticut River, especially at Morgan's coffee house, an establishment run by J.P. Morgan's grandfather. It served as both a club and chamber of commerce, where important business matters were discussed and decided, and the proprietor's advice and assistance always sought.

Agreements were made to share risks and profits on cargos of ships going forth to trade overseas. Until the successful completion of the Revolution, the risk takers were hampered by the fact that specie was scarce. As a result, they often were forced to resort to barter . . . a very awkward method of doing business.

In 1791 the new Congress authorized the establishment of a U.S. Bank with branches to be opened in eligible cities. Hartford merchants, led by Colonel Jeremiah Wadsworth, a personal friend of Alexander Hamilton, justly considered that a commercial bank with the legal right to print money would be particularly beneficial to the economic development of the city. The following year Hartford's first bank, now the Connecticut National Bank, was chartered with a capitalization of $100,000. Besides Wadsworth, the new bank's promoters included Noah Webster, the great lexicographer, and John Caldwell, Samuel Colt's grandfather, who became the first president when Wadsworth declined the position. The Hartford Bank was the first in the new nation to keep its accounts in dollars and cents rather than in pounds and pence.

In 1794 Colonel Wadsworth and three other men of financial substance and moral integrity also pioneered an informal fire insurance con-

Colonel Jeremiah Wadsworth and his son Daniel, first president of the Society for Savings. Oil on canvas.

cern. It was a partnership of gentlemen, and the insuring partners changed as some withdrew and others joined. In every case the partners' personal fortunes were pledged to pay claims in the event of losses.

These casual arrangements soon led to the formation of the first insurance corporation in Connecticut. In May of 1810, the General Assembly gave a charter to the Hartford Fire Insurance Company with a working capital of $15,000. The following month the stockholders held their first meeting at Ransom's Inn. Nine years later, in 1819, a second fire insurance company was organized, the Aetna Fire. Until the 1830s their growth was slow and painful. Twice Hartford Fire saw its surplus swept away by losses.

The concept of fire and marine insurance was not confined to Hartford. The uniqueness of Hartford's companies lay in building a solid reputation for staying solvent, keeping their promises to pay losses, hanging on in times of disaster and initiating new types of insurance. Since "keeping up" has been so vital to the growth of insurance in this city, it is not surprising that local companies pioneered a great number of "firsts" by anticipating changing social conditions without abandoning their basic insistence on absolute fiscal integrity. These "firsts" include the first travelers, steam boiler, automobile and airplane insurance, and the first insurance policy for astronauts.

The tendency of Hartford's Congregational businessmen and bankers to favor one another in their various enterprises was much resented by those who belonged to other denominations. In 1814 this fact inspired the founding of Hartford's second commercial bank, the Phoenix, which later merged with the Connecticut Bank and Trust Company. According to tradition, a prominent founder of this new bank was an irate Episcopalian who had experienced difficulties doing business with the flourishing Hartford Bank. The petitioners for the new bank quite reasonably contended that: ". . . it was more congenial to true republican principles . . . that a new bank be granted (a charter) . . . thereby promoting competition which creates an increasing endeavour to accommodate the public. . . ."

The Panic of 1814, which caused widespread financial ruin, made banks very unpopular. Hence the founders of Connecticut's first mutual savings bank, when they petitioned the General Assembly for a charter in April 1819, avoided the word altogether. They called it instead a "society" for savings and stressed its potential for services to the poor and less fortunate members of the community. The first article of its bylaws clearly stated its purpose:

"The primary objectives of the institution are to aid the industrious, economical and worthy; to protect them from the extravagances of the profligate, the snares of the vicious and to bless them with competency, respectability and happiness."

The 41 prominent citizens who gathered at Ransom's Inn, a popular hostelry, to form the Society for Savings were common-sense Yankees concerned about the welfare of the first wave of immigrants. Most of the newcomers were poor folk from country districts of New England, the British Isles or Europe, strangers to urban living and mercantile values.

Society's first treasurer, Elisha Colt, a cousin of Samuel Colt, was a prominent businessman and politician noted for his broad smile and kindly disposition. Since at the time he was also comptroller of the state of Connecticut, his office in the Old State House became the Society's first headquarters. At the close of business on July 14, the first day, 32

Society for Savings in 1834.

deposits had been made, totaling $532. Mr. Colt is reputed to have kept all deposits in a pocket of his tightly buttoned coat. Whether true or not, three years elapsed before the trustees allocated $30 to buy "a suitable box or trunk for valuables." Later that year Colt moved the bank's headquarters to his home at 10 Church Street. His salary was $90, the rest of the officers serving as volunteers. By 1824 he was paid all of $332, office rent included.

As its assets grew, the Society needed a permanent location, and in 1833 a site on Pratt Street, just north of Bull's Tavern, was selected. Plans for the building were drawn by Daniel Wadsworth. It was completed in 1834 at a cost of $2,500. In the course of the next six decades two new buildings were erected on the same site. Since then Society's headquarters has been remodeled and enlarged many times, but it has always remained the "Pratt Street Bank."

As a philanthropic enterprise, Society endeavored to teach its depositors habits of thrift, serving "seamen bound on a voyage," soldiers, unschooled factory workers, widows and children. One early depositor who took to heart his childhood lessons in the management of money was J.P. Morgan. In 1837 his father Junius opened Account #6835 for his infant son, who grew up to become the nation's greatest financier.

Some 19th century Hartford banks tended to reflect the political as well as religious preferences of their founders. For example, the Farmers' and Mechanics' Bank founded in 1833 was pro-Jackson while the Exchange Bank founded the following year was anti-Jackson. Other banks sprang up during periods of prosperity, and some went out of existence or amalgamated with stronger banks during bad times.

In December of 1835 Hartford made insurance history when a disastrous fire broke out in New York City. Nearly 700 buildings were destroyed. When Eliphalet Terry, president of Hartford Fire, received news of this calamity, he rushed to the Hartford Bank to make sure that all drafts made on his company would be honored. He pledged his personal fortune to cover possible debts and was certain that all members of his board of directors would do likewise. Then, despite the freezing weather, he took off for New York in a horse-drawn sleigh. When he arrived, he found that most other insurance companies had collapsed under the burden of gigantic claims. The burnt-out populace was in despair, believing all insurance policies to be worthless. To the unhappy homeowners and merchants Terry made the dramatic announcement that the "Hartford" stood ready to pay all claims in full. Confidence was restored. Hartford's reputation for reliability burgeoned, and Mr. Terry did not return to his hometown until he had sold a large amount of new insurance!

The success of Mr. Terry's ride stimulated the creation of new insurance companies. Connecticut Mutual Life was founded in 1846, the oldest life insurance company in Connecticut and the sixth oldest in the nation. In 1851 one of the company's founders, Barzillai Hudson, became a founder and first president of the Phoenix Life Insurance Company. The original name of Phoenix was the American Temperance Life Insurance Company. All policyholders were required to sign a pledge promising to totally abstain from drinking any alcoholic beverages. However, the company did not prosper until the pledge requirement was dropped and the name changed.

Connecticut Mutual's first president, Eliphalet A. Bulkeley, became a founder and first president of the Aetna Life Insurance Company (now Aetna Life & Casualty) in 1853. The Travelers Insurance Company was founded in 1864, and Connecticut General Life Insurance Company . . . now CIGNA . . . a year later. Hartford's insurance companies are correctly proud of their fiscal integrity and institutional survival. However, two did fail—the Charter Oak Life Insurance Company in 1878 and the Continental Life Insurance Company in 1887. Others have been merged into their larger brethren, like Phoenix Fire into The Travelers and Aetna Fire into Connecticut General.

In 1845, ten years after Eliphalet Terry's sleigh ride to burning New York City, the same scene was repeated in the same city. Again, Hartford companies kept their promises. In October of 1871, when fire swept through the west side of Chicago like a whirlwind, over 17,000 buildings were reduced to ashes and 250 people killed before the fire could be controlled. As soon as telegraphed dispatches about the holocaust appeared in the *Courant,* insurance executives, anxious for the latest news, jammed into the paper's tiny office on Pratt Street. On October 10 President George L. Chase of the Hartford Fire Insurance Company, wired his agents: "The old Hartford will promptly meet its obligations in Chicago and elsewhere as usual. Continue business and advance rates 50 to 100 percent."

Former Governor Marshall Jewell, a large stockholder and director

Eliphalet A. Bulkeley.
Daquerreotype, c. 1853.

Phoenix Insurance Company advertising poster. Chromolithograph, 1866.

of Phoenix Fire, happened to be in Detroit. Rushing to Chicago, he ran into E.J. Bassett, general agent for Aetna Fire. Together they viewed the ruins. Before an hysterical crowd Jewell mounted a box and announced that Phoenix would pay on the spot any claim that could be substantiated. A Phoenix agent came forward with one, and Jewell wrote out a draft for $10,000. Bassett followed suit for Aetna by signing a check to the amount of $7,750.

The burden of paying off the losses in the Chicago Fire was a heavy one. Aetna Insurance Company, then one of the largest of the fire insurers, paid out $3.75 million, thus sweeping away its capital. Its stock fell sharply from $240 to $50 a share. Hartford Fire lost more than all its assets, nearly $2 million. Connecticut Mutual and the Hartford Bank came to its rescue with a loan of $700,000 and $500,000 in new stock which was subscribed by investors with faith in the future. Phoenix Fire, which lost over a million dollars, also restored its capital by selling additional stock. Obviously with only the dollar in mind, Charles Hopkins Clark, later editor of the *Hartford Courant,* said the suffering in Hartford was "second only to that in Chicago itself." Property losses in the windy city amounted to more than $100 million, and the 200 fire insurance companies involved could pay off only one half of that amount. Sixty-eight insurance companies (outside of Hartford) never recovered.

A year later a conflagration in Boston destroyed nearly 800 buildings in the business district. This time, although more heavily at risk than in Chicago, most of the Hartford insurers came through in good shape. Aetna Insurance Company was the exception, losing more than $1.6 million and making necessary the issuance of $2.5 million in new stock to keep the company afloat.

In 1906, after the San Francisco earthquake and fire, insurance claims were truly staggering. In the U.S. Senate one senator sadly commented that no American fire insurance company now could possibly be sure of solvency. Challenged, Morgan G. Bulkeley, senator from Connecticut and president of the Aetna Life Insurance Company, rose quickly to his feet. He pointed proudly to Hartford's history of reliability and then added fiercely, "I do unhesitatingly affirm that Hartford companies will pay in full every claim made against them."

And they did—thanks to the loyal support of Hartford banks and other local insurance companies.

The Hartford Steam Boiler Inspection and Insurance Company owes its origin directly to the widespread use of steam power to operate factories in general and, specifically, because of a boiler explosion in Hartford at the Fales & Gray Car Works that killed 21 workers and injured 50 more. In 1857 a small group interested in the mystery of boiler explosions and anxious to improve their safety founded the Polytechnic Club. Explosions were then occurring with alarming frequency and most people accepted them as "acts of God." The effort of the Club members to form a company to inspect and insure boilers, as already existed in England, was cut short by the onset of the Civil War. But in 1866 a charter was granted to Hartford Steam Boiler, which by the turn of the century had become the undisputed leader in its field.

The stability of Hartford insurance companies has redounded to the benefit of their employees during nation-wide crises. The firms managed to survive the Great Depression of 1930 and two world wars with a minimum of dislocation. In 1933 the impact of the bank moratorium was cushioned when the life companies became the sole source for cash

Traveler's Tower, December 1940.

payments. Most of their people were kept employed. Aetna Life, for example, laid off nobody during the Depression. Salaries were reduced only once, when the cost of living fell to such a degree that the cut was balanced by the increase in purchasing power.

Hartford insurance companies played a key role during World War II in the development of the "Manhattan Project." In summing up the experience, an Army spokesman asserted that "the cooperation of the interested insurance carriers . . . contributed materially to the successful completion of the atomic bomb by making available to the contractors unusual insurance coverage."

In the mid 1950s Travelers and other Hartford insurance companies, thanks to their experience with the "Manhattan Project," began to play an essential role in the development of atomic power for peacetime use. The exploration of outer space also has mandated innovative insurance coverage.

Today Hartford is much more than just "the insurance city" of the nation. With its large banks and multinational insurance companies, it has become a major financial center. The 46 insurance companies that presently have their home offices in Greater Hartford have world-wide assets of $119.3 billion. Every day $72 million comes into the city in insurance premiums, and more than $17 billion a year is paid out in benefits and claims. Altogether, these companies constitute the second largest private employer in the state. Even more significant to the economy as a whole are the massive nation-wide investments made by Hartford insurance firms—investments that now total almost a trillion dollars!

The most visible evidence of their commitment to the viability of the downtown area is the rapidly changing skyline. Following the completion of the "Gold Building" on Main Street and the Civic Center in the middle '70s, seven large office towers have risen, adding nearly eight million square feet of office space. Many other older buildings have been rehabilitated. By the end of 1986 an additional 1.6 million square feet of new or renovated space will be completed.

The Civic Center, with its variety of restaurants and stores, has attracted increasing numbers of shoppers, diners and sports fans to downtown, spurring a retail renaissance in the city. Through the promotional efforts of the Greater Hartford Convention and Visitors Bureau, the Downtown Council and the Civic Center, Hartford is becoming a popular place to conduct regional and national conventions.

Hartford Insurance Firsts

Accident insurance
Automobile policies
Aviation policies
Renewal term life insurance plan
Rain insurance
Training school for agents and field representatives
Group paid-up life insurance
Industrial engineering department to reduce number and severity of accidents
Group cost-of-living-at-work plan
Double indemnity life insurance to provide added benefits in the event of death by accident
Life insurance for astronauts in space

Detail of lithograph of Hartford showing the Park River and Rifle Avenue (now Capitol Avenue), 1864.

HARTFORD IRON FOUNDRY.

The undersigned will execute to order, all kinds of IRON CASTINGS that may be required;---their assortment of Patterns is extensive, embracing most kinds of machinery now in use. High pressure STEAM ENGINES. PLOUGH CASTINGS of all kinds, constantly on hand. Being joint owners with B. Lyman, in his Patent for CAST IRON WHEEL HUBS---and General Agents for the United States, they are now prepared to furnish them for all kinds of Carriages, Waggons, Drays, Carts, &c.---The rapidly increasing use of this article is its best recommendation.---Orders from any part of the country will be promptly attended to :---prices same as at New-York, Boston and Philadelphia.

A. & T. HANKS.

Hartford, Conn. *A.D. 1821.*

Hartford Iron Foundry
broadside.
Lithograph, 1821.

The Rise of Manufacturing

As early as 1787 Connecticut's delegation to the Constitutional Convention in Philadelphia announced to assembled members: "We represent a manufacturing state." This pronouncement was more prophecy than fact, agriculture and trade actually being the basis of the state's economy. However, after the Revolution and the disastrous War of 1812, Connecticut's wise leaders knew that, if their state was to compete successfully with others in the Union, the promotion of manufacturing was essential.

Manufacturing required power. The most primitive sources of power, muscles of men and beasts, wind and water, were first utilized. Very soon after the settlement of Hartford, grist and saw mills were built on the Little River, subsequently known as the Mill, Hog and Park River. These names were most descriptive of its fate, for it originally served as a source of power, then as an open sewer for industrial wastes. When Horace Bushnell inspired the creation of Bushnell Park, the river's name was appropriately changed. Today it has almost disappeared within the city since most of its waters are conducted through underground culverts into the Connecticut River.

In the old days both overshot and undershot water wheels on local streams supplied most of the power used. For instance, George Goodwin's mill in what is now East Hartford furnished paper for the *Connecticut Courant,* of which Goodwin was co-publisher. On the Park River, water power ran the Hartford Woolen Manufactory. Except for the C.H. Dexter paper mill in Windsor Locks, no local enterprise used water for power directly from the Connecticut River.

After the Revolution British manufacturers did their best to suppress any American industry that might compete with their exports to the new nation. At first Americans lacked the basic ingredients that gave birth to the Industrial Revolution in England: capital, skilled labor, complex machinery and an efficient system of distribution. The state's many "homespun" industries provided local folk with most of their necessities. But village workshops, utilizing waterpower, were unable to become real factories until the advent of the steam engine.

Until the 1830s, therefore, there was only minimal growth of manufacturing in the Hartford area, especially as compared to such communities as New Haven (arms), Waterbury (brass), New Britain (hardware) and Plymouth (clocks). The city's economy was still river-oriented, but new enterprises were adding to its prosperity. In 1820, when the population totaled around 7,000, there were, besides several blacksmiths and cabinetmakers, three cotton and woolen mills, six tanneries, five potteries, two tin shops, 15 shoemakers, six book binderies, eight distilleries, two hat shops, two looking-glass makers and four coppersmiths.

The introduction of steam power after 1815 revolutionized not only transportation on land and water but also accelerated the growth of manufacturing and completely changed the living style of workers. Mills and factories, using stationary steam engines, could be located anywhere, and the city was the logical place because of the proximity of the labor supply. In turn, the factories attracted hordes of newcomers. Hartford rapidly became urbanized, nearly doubling in size from 1820 to 1840 and more than doubling from 1840 to 1860, with clusters of multistoried factories, smoking chimneys and dingy slums nearby.

ABOVE,
G. Goodwin & Sons Mill,
East Hartford.
Engraved label.

Among the earliest users of steam were the brothers Alpheus and Truman Hanks, who started the Hartford Iron Foundry in 1820. Noted for making the first cast iron plow, this foundry later became Woodruff & Beach, famous for its steam engines. Among their achievements were a gigantic 250-horsepower engine for Sam Colt's Armory and a double-piston pump for the Hartford Water Works. Considered an engineering marvel in 1855, this pump lifted water from the Connecticut River all the way up to the public reservoir on Lord's Hill, now the site of the Hartford Insurance Group. Hartford residents drank river water until 1876 when the Connecticut became too polluted and new reservoirs had to be built in West Hartford.

The lifeline between steam engine and machinery was the leather belt. The old Jewell Belting Company, founded by Pliny Jewell in 1845, made leather belts of all sizes for Hartford's plants. Jewell was the third such enterprise in the nation and, for many years, the largest belting company in the world.

Without energy and the machine there would have been no Industrial Revolution, nor would the United States have become the leading industrial society. Our industrial strength can be attributed to the mastery of precision metal working and, in particular, to the rapid growth of the machine tool industry beginning in the middle of the last century. A significant part of that growth took place in New England—mainly in Windsor, Vermont; Providence, Rhode Island; and Hartford, Connecticut. The machine tool, which creates all other tools and even replicates itself, enabled the system of interchangeable parts invented by Eli Whitney of Hamden and Simeon North of Berlin to be brought to a state of perfection, which in turn made possible the spread of mass production for every conceivable human need.

The patron saint of American machine tools was Eli Whitney, who in 1818 developed a plain milling machine for rotary cutting. Thirty years later it was improved substantially by Frederick W. Howe in Vermont. Then the action moved to the Sharps Rifle Company in Hartford. The start-up of this factory in 1852 to manufacture Christian Sharps' rifle opened up what became the Capitol Avenue industrial cen-

Colt's Patent Firearms Manufactory. Lithograph.

ter that would subsequently accommodate such great enterprises as Weed Sewing Machine, Pope Manufacturing, Pratt & Whitney Machine Tools, Arrow Hart & Hegeman, Underwood Typewriter, and Hartford Machine Screw. For a long while Capitol Avenue was called Rifle Avenue.

To Sharps, Richard S. Lawrence brought the Howe miller, which caused a sensation among Hartford mechanics. A gifted young man named Francis A. Pratt refined the basic design in 1855, creating the famous Lincoln miller, some 200,000 of which were eventually sold. In the South Meadows, at the same point in time, Colonel Samuel Colt, the city's first real tycoon, had just completed his great Armory. Here a Woodruff & Beach steam engine, with a 30-foot flywheel, ran hundreds of gun-making machines by means of Jewell's leather belts. It also heated the entire plant. Colt gave the world much more than the six-shot revolver that won the West and revolutionized techniques of warfare. In the imposing, onion-domed factory his brilliant superintendent, Elisha K. Root, took giant strides toward perfecting the Whitney-North system of interchangeability. Probably the ablest mechanic who ever lived in New England, the quiet, soft-spoken Root excelled as a teacher. Under him at various times worked such achievers as Francis Pratt, Amos Whitney, Charles E. Billings, Christopher Spencer and George A. Fairfield, all of whom "graduated" to found metal-working companies of their own in Hartford.

The Armory became a training center for the mechanical arts at a time when the only way to learn them was by serving as apprentices and understudies. Had the city fathers not enraged Colt by their arrogant contempt for his development of what amounted to a model manufacturing community, complete with roads, utilities, employee boarding houses, and recreational facilities like Charter Oak Hall, he would have left a quarter of his fortune for the establishment of an engineering school that would surely have rivaled M.I.T. or Rensselaer.

A millionaire at age 40, Colonel Colt built, at his own expense, the city's first dikes to keep spring floods from inundating his property near the river. He also paid good wages, but sternly expected top-notch workmanship in return. On the west boundary of his park he built his mansion, Armsmear. Now greatly altered in appearance, the main part,

RIGHT,
Armsmear.

Sam Colt.
Engraving, c. 1860.

fronting on Wethersfield Avenue, is preserved as an historic landmark and is also a home for widows of Episcopal ministers.

Worn out by his labors, Colt died in his 47th year in 1862. As a memorial to her husband and their four children who died in infancy, Mrs. Colt erected the Church of the Good Shepherd in the middle of Colt Park. Designed by Edward Tuckerman Potter, later the architect for the Mark Twain House and the Caldwell Colt Memorial, it is probably the only church in the world with a revolver motif. Tucked among the crosses and the capitals of the columns that adorn the southeast entrance are parts of guns, bullet molds and machine screws.

The first labor organizations in Hartford were mechanics' associations, comprised of journeymen and apprentices and dominated by their masters. In 1816 the Mechanics Society of Hartford was founded to aid disabled members, their widows and orphans. During the Jacksonian era industrial workers became more class-conscious and reform-minded. Their cause was promoted by the Democratic press, especially the *Times,* whose editor attacked sweatshop employers and the moneyed aristocracy. One of the first labor disputes in America took place in Thompsonville in 1833, when fiercely independent Scottish weavers struck for higher piece rates. In 1836 appeared the first trade union, the Journeymen Carpenters and Joiners Society, which fought for the 10-hour day, a reform adopted in 1855 but not enforced until 1887.

At the same time considerable attention was paid to worker education. The Hartford Mechanics' Society offered lectures and maintained a library. The "Ciceronian Lyceum" sponsored discussions of vital interest to workingmen, such as imprisonment for debt and universal suffrage. The combination of agitation and education resulted in a flood of reforms being adopted by the Legislature, most notably a limited mechanics' lien law and the abolition of imprisonment for debt.

The rapid growth of manufacturing after 1850 spurred the development of a trade unionism concerned primarily with wages, hours and working conditions. In Connecticut the carpetweavers, cigar makers, printers, and hatmakers became affiliated with strong national unions. Union influence on labor legislation reached a high point in 1885-1886 when the General Assembly passed acts limiting child labor and hours worked and providing for factory inspections and weekly payment of wages earned. Mainly through the efforts of Hartford's Central Labor Union, a Connecticut branch of the American Federation of Labor was formed in 1887.

In 1901 Hartford experienced its only city-wide walkout over the issues of the nine-hour day and union recognition. That spring 50,000 members of the International Association of Machinists went on strike across the country. In Hartford some 2,500 joined them, led by the workers at Pratt & Whitney and Electric Vehicle. Only Colt's 750 employees stayed on the job. It took the president of the Central Labor Union, Ignatius Sullivan, to bring about peace. A persuasive Irishman from the East Side, he talked the employers into sitting down with shop committees of their own employees, without the presence of union leaders, and resolving their differences. As a result, agreement was reached on 10 hours' pay for nine hours of work. Sullivan's successful mediation was responsible for his becoming mayor the next year.

Despite these gains Hartford remained an open-shop bastion until the advent of the New Deal. Today some 50 union organizations are located in the Hartford area.

After the Civil War the Weed Sewing Machine Company settled

Christopher Spencer, 1918.
BELOW,
Manufacture of bicycles at the Weed Sewing Machine Factory, 1880.

down on Capitol Avenue and soon became, next to Colt's, the largest manufacturer in the city. From 1876 to 1881 George Fairfield served as Weed's president, during which period occurred two events that had a significant impact on the future of metal working as well as on Hartford's industrial prosperity. One was the fortuitous meeting with Colonel Albert A. Pope of Boston which quickly led to Weed's entry into making Pope's "Columbia" high-wheel bicycle, the first commercial self-propelled vehicle in America. By 1890, the sewing machine market having collapsed, Weed made nothing but safety bicycles; Colonel Pope assumed complete control and changed the firm's name to the Pope Manufacturing Company.

The other event was the coming together of the inventor Christopher Spencer and Fairfield in 1873 over the former's latest and, as it turned out, most epochal invention. Inside the Weed factory the genius from Manchester built the first single-spindle automatic screw machine. It proved to be the birth of not only the screw machine industry in America but, three years later, resulted in the founding of Hartford Machine Screw, now a division of Stanadyne in Windsor.

The progress in interchangeability of machine parts made by Root at the Colt Armory was extended further by Francis Pratt and Amos Whitney in their machine tool enterprise, begun in 1860. Prior to 1900 the partners designed an astonishing variety of machines—lathes, boring mills, shapers, planers, vertical drills, grinders, die sinkers, profilers, presses, power hammers and various cutting machines. No other machine tool builder, before or since, could match this record. Before World War I, Pratt & Whitney Machine Tool was the largest company of its kind. Like Root, Amos Whitney also excelled in teaching hundreds of apprentices to become journeymen and to start other businesses.

William Gray, a mechanic at the old Pratt & Whitney Machine Tool Company on Capitol Avenue, invented and patented the first coin-operated telephone in 1889, thus making a major contribution to the communications revolution. With the assistance of local businessmen, he founded the Gray Pay Station Telephone Company. That same year, a pay telephone was installed on the lines of the Southern New England Company.

In 1897 Colonel Pope and Hiram P. Maxim, the inventor, made his-

George J. Mead, Frederick B. Rentschler, Donald L. Brown and employee inspect the 1000th Wasp engine, c. 1927–29.

tory when they offered to the public the first electric carriage in America. Under the headline "Horseless Era Comes," the *Courant* welcomed the Mark III car which had an operating radius of 30 miles and a top speed of 12 miles an hour. The following year Maxim had on the road a four-wheel vehicle with a two-cylinder air-cooled engine that traveled from Hartford to Boston, with repeated stops due to frightened horses and dreadful roads.

Had Henry Ford remained a farmer, the capital of Connecticut might also have become the automobile capital of the United States instead of Detroit. Having acquired the Selden patent in the expectation that it would give them a stranglehold on the internal combustion engine, Pope, his dynamic associate George H. Day and his New York backers determined to put the "cocky" upstart from Detroit out of business. In 1903 they filed suit against Ford, a litigation that dragged on for eight years and ended in a victory for Henry Ford. By that time Pope Manufacturing had failed, and both its founder and George Day were dead.

Hartford made up for it by becoming the number one manufacturer of aircraft engines. In 1925 Frederick Rentschler and George Mead designed and built the first successful air-cooled airplane engine, the renowned Wasp, in the old Pratt & Whitney complex on Capitol Avenue. Today Pratt & Whitney Aircraft is a division of United Technologies.

Between 1860 and 1960 Hartford inventors and entrepreneurs established the city as the foremost manufacturing center in New England. Through brainpower they overcame the state's lack of natural resources. From the opening of the U.S. Patent Office in 1790 until 1930 Connecticut received more patents per capita than any other state, about one per thousand citizens. Apparently, there was only one thing a Yankee could not invent even if he put his hand to it; over the grave of Jonathan Kilbourne in Colchester is this epitaph:

"He was a man of invention great
Above all that liv'd nigh;
But he could not invent to live
When God called him to die."

New forms of energy undergirded Yankee ingenuity. After steam power came gas for illumination in 1848, then electricity in the 1880s, generated by the burning of coal and oil. Then in 1962 the first atomic power plant was built on the Connecticut River at Haddam Neck by the Hartford Electric Light and Connecticut Light & Power utilities, now part of Northeast Utilities.

The 1950s and 1960s were notable for major shifts in the demographic and economic bases of the city and its suburbs. Between 1950 and 1980 the city lost more than 40,000 people, declining from a peak of 177,000 to 136,000. In the same period the nine surrounding towns grew from 127,000 to nearly 288,000, more than double the number left in the city. Avon and Simsbury are now the fastest growing towns in the region.

The decline in Hartford's population left the core city with a large number of blacks and Hispanics, many of whom lacked the education and technical know-how to find employment. Because of this situation Hartford was ranked as the fourth poorest city in the nation, yet between 1960 and 1980 the number of jobs generated downtown rose from 115,840 to 143,180—jobs mandating a white-collar work force. While city residents filled nearly half of the available jobs in 1960, only 23 percent did so 20 years later.

Furthermore, the factories which for 100 years had provided plenty of entry-level work were disappearing. Employing more people than the insurance companies, they had been turning out such varied products as horseshoe nails, counters, organs, pay telephones, machine tools, screw machine products, electric switches, Colt guns and Maxim silencers, and glass-blowing machinery. As their multistoried buildings became obsolete, many found it necessary to move where there was ample space for more efficient one-story operation and for employee parking. Others went out of business or left the state entirely—like Fuller brushes and Royal and Underwood typewriters—eliminating over 10,000 jobs. As a result, the majority of jobs are now to be found in the insurance, finance, distribution and government sectors.

Looking at the 33 towns of the Capitol Region as an entity, it might appear that Hartford is an economic island in the middle of a suburban sea. Of the nearly 400,000 persons in this labor market, about 40 percent work in the city itself. In the past decade alone manufacturing, including the thousands employed at Pratt & Whitney Aircraft in East Hartford, declined 31 percent to 25 percent of the total employment. Within the nonmanufacturing sectors there were sharp increases in those employed in government (20 percent), insurance (39 percent), retail and wholesale trade (31 percent), and finance and real estate. Historically, the Capitol Region has enjoyed a lower unemployment rate than either the state or the nation, and the demand for skilled workers to fill the available jobs in the expanding high technology and service industries continues unabated.

Greater Hartford has the distinction of being the second largest retail shopping area in New England. Nine of the largest industrial corporations and six of the largest insurance companies are headquartered here. A number of foreign companies operate in the area, with representation from Canada, Belgium, West Germany, Switzerland, France and the United Kingdom. The median age of its 174,000 families, 32 years, is younger than the state's or the nation's. Levels of education are also higher than elsewhere. Nearly 60 percent are high school graduates and 15 percent college graduates. One in three is employed in a professional or managerial occupation. Greater Hartford has been ranked first among all 50 states in its quality-of-living environment.

As a state, Connecticut on a per capita basis outproduces all other countries in the world. The output of more than $50 billion worth of goods annually gives the state the 38th largest economy in the world—larger than the countries of Finland, Taiwan, Greece and Egypt. Dividing its production by its population of 3.1 million results in a per capita rating of $16,396—higher than second-ranked Saudi Arabia and third-ranked Switzerland.

Major Hartford Inventors and Business Achievements		
	1788	First woolen mill in United States.
	1794	Smith, Brown & Co. established the first saddlery, oldest in the nation.
	1797	Apollos Kinsley's steam wagon.
	1820	Alpheus & Truman Hanks made first iron plow castings.
	1829	Henry Hudson's introduction of the Fourdrinier machine to make paper.

1836	Alonzo D. Phillips' patent for friction matches. Samuel Colt obtained patent for his revolver.
1845	Jewell Belting Company founded.
1846	Invention of electroplating machine by Rogers brothers.
1852	Christian Sharps' rifle.
1855	Francis Pratt's Lincoln miller. Opening of Colt's Armory. A.P. Pitkin introduced galvanized piping for water systems.
1857	Gyroscopes made in Hartford. First brick machine installed in Hartford. Pitkin brothers responsible for first machine-made watch.
1862	Formation of Cushman Chuck Company.
1865	Publication of first house organ or industrial magazine by The Travelers.
1865	Linus Plimpton began manufacture of envelopes.
1873	Christopher Spencer's invention of the automatic screw machine.
1878	Columbia bicycle produced by Weed Sewing Machine.
1879	Smyth Manufacturing the first to sew books by machine.
1881	George J. Capewell's invention of horseshoe nail machinery.
1884	Moses Johnson invented the friction clutch.
1885	Perfection by Pratt & Whitney of a standard measuring machine accurate to 1/100,000th of an inch.
1886	William Gray's invention of coin-operated telephone.
1888	Pope's safety bicycle launched.
1894	Curtis Veeder's invention of the cyclometer.
1895	First pneumatic tire for automobiles.
1897	Pope Manufacturing Company's electric automobile.
1899	John T. Austin invented the air chest organ.
1901	Underwood Typewriter moved to Hartford. Hartford Electric Light Company the first utility to install a steam turbine generator.
1906	Founding of Fuller Brush Company.
1909	Hiram Maxim's invention of a gun silencer.
1917	John Browning perfected the machine gun, automatic rifle and automatic pistol.
1918	Karl Peiler's invention of an automatic bottle-making machine.
1933	Veeder Root introduced gasoline pump counter.
1943	Gray Manufacturing made first radar set.
1953	Dr. Vernon Krieble invented the anaerobic adhesive.
1969	Hamilton Standard developed space suits for astronauts.
1984	Propulsion units made by Hamilton Standard to retrieve satellites in space.

Columbia Bicycle catalog cover, 1880.

5   A City of the World

Hartford today is cosmopolitan, American to the core, yet embracing almost every culture and nationality in the world. Strange to say, this delightfully pluralistic city was founded 350 years ago by English Puritans as a deliberately *exclusive* community. Hartford's transformation to *inclusiveness* is a dramatic saga and a tribute to Yankee idealism and common sense.

Like the ancient Jews in the Old Testament, who were their role models, the Puritans excluded all who did not share their religious convictions. Their aspiration was to build here in the wilderness a New Jerusalem . . . a city on a hill that would be an example of Christian excellence to all mankind. So those belonging to other nations or religions were definitely unwelcome. Even other Protestant Englishmen, like Quakers and Episcopalians, were discouraged from settling permanently in the Connecticut Colony, which originally consisted of Hartford, Windsor and Wethersfield. The Congregational was the established church and none other was allowed.

Despite their conservatism, Connecticut's first settlers were extremely adventuresome as merchants and traders. First, of course, they had to make peace with the local Suckiaug Indians, who were friendly, and the dominant Pequots, who were not. The military victory over the latter in 1637 brought about peace and stability at least until King Philip's War in 1675–1676.

Another short-term threat was the Dutch who in 1633 had established a fur trading post in an area still called Dutch Point, but who peacefully withdrew in 1654.

After their little settlement was firmly established, the Puritans turned their attention to economic growth. It is no accident that the first American-built vessel to trade in the West Indies was constructed in Wethersfield in 1649. Soon sea captains and merchants from the river ports of Hartford, Windsor and Wethersfield were actively involved in trade all along the Atlantic coast, with the mother country, and with the West Indies and Africa. The latter included the slave trade.

Although Connecticut captains sold many slaves in the Indies and southern colonies, slavery within the colony was never very widespread for practical rather than moral reasons. Connecticut farms, unlike the huge plantations in the South and Caribbean, tended to be small and family operated, and Africans were employed chiefly as house servants and occasionally as farm hands.

Blacks, mulattoes and Indians in colonial Connecticut had no political power. Although not *legally* denied the right to participate in politics, they were barred by custom and tradition. One exception was Frank Freeman who was elected to a minor political office in the town of Farmington in the 1670s. Black males, however, were encouraged to vote on "Lection Day," a mock election that took place every year on the Saturday following the real general election. On this occasion a black "Governor" would be chosen. He and his aides and constituents, elaborately dressed, took part in a grand inauguration that terminated in feasting and games. A particularly popular "Governor" was Peleg Nott, the slave of Colonel Jeremiah Wadsworth of Hartford.

Since blacks seldom attended the common schools, they were prevented from learning how to read and write unless instructed by their owners. Even so, some ambitious men managed to become skilled barbers, tailors, masons, carpenters, brick makers, iron workers, shoemakers, wagoners and stoneworkers. One outstanding black man was a slave named Primus. Reputed to have been a prince in Africa, he was brought to this country in the 18th century and purchased by Dr. Alexander Wolcott of Windsor. Impressed by his intelligence, Wolcott trained him as his assistant. This was the custom in those days, there being no medical schools. The young African eventually became so skilled that his master freed him. Then, as Dr. Primus, he set up a thriving practice in what is now South Windsor. In the 19th century one of his descendants, Holdridge Primus, acquired a considerable financial interest in a grocery store on Main Street in Hartford. His son, Nelson Primus, became a popular portrait painter.

Lemuel Haynes was born in what is now West Hartford in 1753. His father was an African and his mother a member of a prominent white family. His white grandfather sent the mulatto infant to Granville, Massachusetts, where he was raised by a pious deacon and his wife in their family of five children. Haynes received an excellent education and proved to be an outstanding scholar. He eventually became a widely respected Congregational minister and was the first black in New England to preach regularly to white congregations.

As early as 1660, laws were passed exempting black males from military duty and forbidding them to own weapons. No doubt the whites feared that the guns might be used against them! Many black men, however, did participate in Connecticut's Colonial wars, and some received their freedom for their services. When the American Revolution broke out in 1775, approximately 6,464 persons of African heritage were residents. In fact, Connecticut had more black residents than any other colony in New England—3.2 percent of the total population, and 2.3 percent of Hartford's residents. Like most of their white neighbors,

Lemuel Haynes.
Engraving, c. 1837.

many black Yankees, among them Lemuel Haynes, responded eagerly to the call for troops. During the war a company of black infantrymen attached to Butler's Regiment of the Connecticut line saw active service. This was probably the first organization of black troops in the U.S. military forces.

Connecticut Indians, often intermarried with blacks, also took part in the Revolutionary War. Samson Occum, for example, who eventually became a Congregational minister, and his brother-in-law, Jacob Fowler, were patriotic Mohegans. Fowler, a teacher at the Rev. Eleazer Wheelock's Indian School, served as a trusted military courier for Connecticut's Governor Jonathan Trumbull throughout the rebellion.

By 1774 many people began to look upon slavery as a threat to free labor. An act was passed stating that "no Indian, Negro or Mulatto slave shall be at any time hereafter brought or imported into this colony." One year after the end of the American Revolution, a new Connecticut law stated: "Whereas sound policy requires that the abolition of slavery should be effected as soon as may be consistent with the rights of individuals [which referred to protecting the property rights of slave owners!], therefore be it enacted that no Negro or Mulatto child that shall after the first day of March, 1784, be born within the state shall be held in servitude longer than until they arrive at the age of 25 years."

Although some people disapproved of slaves and freed blacks serving as soldiers, by the end of 1777 they were being actively recruited in Connecticut and a few other states. Some even served in place of the sons and relatives of their masters, their particular reward being freedom when the war ended. Many were cited for outstanding bravery.

Sad to say, these many acts of personal heroism and sacrifice did not substantially improve the status of black men in Connecticut. In 1783 Jupiter Hammon, reputed to be the first American black poet, wrote a poetic dialogue that was printed in Hartford and quite accurately described the continuing relationship between whites and blacks. It was aptly entitled, *The Kind Master and The Dutiful Servant*.

For over 150 years, Connecticut continued to be governed by the old Royal Charter that Governor John Winthrop Jr. had procured from King Charles II in 1662. Responding to the many changes taking place, a new state constitution was adopted in 1818 that disestablished the Congregational Church and allowed all Christian religions to flourish freely. This was a great boon to the Episcopalians, Baptists, Methodists, Presbyterians and Quakers and also to the Roman Catholics who were beginning to come into the state.

Driven to desperation by famine in their mother country, thousands of Irish had begun flocking into the United States in order to survive. The first few hundred to arrive in Hartford had little to offer but strong backs and willing hands. They settled chiefly along Talcott, Front and Market streets and found work constructing the new canal and railroad networks that were essential to Connecticut's emerging manufacturing economy. Many of the women became domestic servants.

From the beginning the poor Irish and Hartford's black residents competed with one another for the least skilled jobs. This led to interpersonal animosities and, sometimes, to open riots. By May of 1823 the Irish were sufficiently numerous to invite Bishop John Chevros of Boston to visit Hartford. The Bishop celebrated Mass in the Old State House and baptized a number of Catholic children. The following month the first Roman Catholic congregation in Hartford was "gathered."

On October 6, 1762, the Episcopalians (Anglicans) purchased a lot in Hartford on Main Street, then called King Street. The lot comprised what would eventually be the northwest corner of Main and Church streets, as the latter was not opened until 1794. Stones were gathered to lay a foundation for the new sanctuary, but the efforts of the Episcopalians were frustrated by the outbreak of the American Revolution. Anti-English and anti-Anglican feelings were intense in fiercely patriotic Connecticut, so Episcopalians often were roughly treated as potential traitors. In Hartford their new lot was illegally confiscated by the town fathers, and a rabid revolutionary named Samuel Talcott stole the building materials they were forced to abandon.

After the war, in 1784, the Episcopalians in Hartford went to court to regain their property. They won their case and soon began to construct their church. There is a tradition that, in 1792, when Prince Brewster, the chief mason of the project and a loyal parish member, was laying the cornerstone, he said to the assembled citizens, "I lay this stone for the foundation of an Episcopal Church, and Sam Talcott and the gates of hell cannot prevail against it."

RIGHT,
First Episcopal and first Roman Catholic church in Hartford, 1876.

In 1829, after completing a new stone church designed by the famous architect, Ithiel Towne, on the southwest corner of Church and Main streets, the Episcopalians sold their former church to the Roman Catholics. On July 10 of that same year, Bishop Benedict J. Fenwick of Boston arrived in Hartford to consummate the purchase. Episcopal Bishop Thomas C. Brownell is reputed to have commented: "Well, Bishop Fenwick, as we have a fine new church building, we will let you have the old one." To which Bishop Fenwick replied, "Yes, Bishop Brownell. And as you have a fine new religion, we will keep the old one!" The Catholics renamed their sanctuary Church of the Holy Trinity and moved it over to Talcott Street, near Front Street, where most of the Irish immigrants were living.

Until the 19th century in Connecticut, blacks worshipped in white churches. The most important members of any community sat in the best pews, while nonwhites were relegated to the back of the church or the gallery.

In 1819 the black communicants of Center Congregational Church in Hartford rebelled against this demeaning custom. Under the leadership of the Rev. Asa Goldborough, they began worshipping together in the church conference room. The following year they established a Sunday School exclusively for "people of color" at the foot of State Street. On May 11, 1826, they formed the African Religious Society of Hartford (Holdridge Primus was a member), purchased land at the corner of Talcott and Market streets, and built a small, wooden meeting house first known as the Talcott Street Church. In 1833 the church was officially recognized by the white Congregationalists. Six years later the name was changed to the First Colored Congregational Church . . . now Faith Congregational Church on Main Street. Church parishioners requested, and were granted, the right to use their church on weekdays as an all-black public school. A similar school was opened in African Methodist Episcopal Church on Pearl Street which had been founded in 1833 . . . now A.M.E. Zion Church on Main Street.

All public schools in those days were extremely spartan and devoid of amenities. However, the condition of the two little schools for black children was deplorable. On October 17, 1846, the Rev. James W.C. Pennington, pastor of the church on Talcott Street, wrote a letter to the *Courant* expressing his dismay. " . . . The colored children in the several districts are numbered with the white children and their head money paid to our committee. The money so received amounts to about half of what is required to support a school continuously. The balance has to be raised by us . . . No school house has been provided other than the vestry of the church which is not only too damp for the purpose, but is now greatly out of repair."

In 1852, after considerable prodding by Pennington and others, a new public school exclusively for black youngsters was constructed on Pearl Street. Blacks in Hartford continued to be educated separately until 1868 when the Legislature finally passed a law requiring all children to attend their own district school regardless of race.

ABOVE,
Talcott Street Congregational Church, 1858.
RIGHT,
The A.M.E. Zion Church (African) built in 1857. Photographed shortly before it was torn down in 1898.

WASHINGTON DAGUERREIAN GALLERY,
NO. 136 MAIN STREET,
(A few doors North of the Centre Church.)

WASHINGTON is at home, and daily executing beautiful and correct Miniatures, equal to any in this country, at his uncommonly cheap prices.

oct 8   12d 4w77

Advertisement for Augustus Washington's daguerreian gallery, 1852.

A native of Trenton, New Jersey, Augustus Washington moved to Hartford in 1844 and became a teacher in one of the city's African schools. Three years later he opened a daguerrean studio on Main Street. His daguerreotypes were of excellent quality, and Hartford's leading citizens were among his patrons.

An unusually well-educated black, Washington suffered acutely from the fact that racial discrimination blocked him from any real opportunities for advancement. In his words: ". . . whatever may be a colored man's capacity and literary attainments . . . as soon as he leaves the academic halls to mingle in the only society he can find in the United States, unless he is a minister or lecturer, he must and will retrograde . . . (and) just in proportion as he increases in knowledge, will he become the more miserable." Washington also was depressed by the political impotence of blacks in this state. In 1818 black men were dealt a cruel blow by a provision in the new Connecticut constitution *legally* denying them the franchise for the first time. This Constitution, otherwise so liberal in that it disestablished the Congregational Church and allowed all Christian religions to flourish, was a major political setback. The insult was compounded in 1847 when a state-wide effort to give the vote to black men was soundly defeated. The following year slavery in Connecticut finally was abolished. By then, however, only six slaves remained to be freed.

Convinced that only Africa could be a black American's real home, Washington migrated to Liberia in 1854. At this time in Hartford, both the colonization and abolition movements were very active.

In 1862, while the Civil War was still raging, two of Hartford's most respected black residents, Prince and John Saunders, both tax-paying property owners, sent a petition to Congress protesting Connecticut's practice of "taxation without representation." Their protest fell on deaf ears. Not until 1876 were black male citizens of this state allowed to participate in the political process. Even so, they still had very little political "clout" since they comprised only about 3 percent of the population.

On March 23, 1790, sixteen city residents organized the First Baptist Church of Hartford (now Central Baptist). The first sanctuary of this denomination literally arrived floating down the Connecticut River during a spring flood! The bouyant building belonged to some upriver Methodists. Because returning the church to its original congregation proved to be very expensive, the thrifty Baptists purchased it from the Methodists and set it up on Market Street where it served their congregation for many years. Around 1830 the Baptists built a fine new church on the present site of the Richardson Building on Main Street.

During the 17th and 18th centuries, a few Sephardic Jews from Spain or Portugal visited Hartford briefly. However, the first Jews to settle down in this city came from Germany during the first half of the 19th century.

RIGHT,
First Baptist Church 1830–1856;
Touro Hall (Congregation Beth Israel), 1856–1876.
BELOW,
Rabbi Isaac Mayer, First Rabbi of Beth Israel 1856–1867.

In 1842 Jews were granted the same degree of religious freedom already given to Christians by the Constitution of 1818. The following year they organized the first Reform Jewish congregation in Hartford, Beth Israel (Home of Israel), which included about 200 people. Their religious headquarters were first on Market Street, then on the corner of Wells and Main streets. In 1856 they purchased the First Baptist Church on Main Street. Renaming the church Touro Hall in honor of the philanthropist Judah Touro, they used the building as a neighborhood center for worship, for public meetings, and for civic and cultural events.

Their first rabbi was Dr. Isaac Mayer. One of the rabbi's sons, Dr. Nathan Mayer, was a surgeon with the Union forces during the Civil War. He also was a writer and a poet. For over 40 years he was the music and drama critic for the *Hartford Times.*

Many German Jews became outstanding citizens of the city of Hartford. Gershon Fox, founder of G. Fox & Co. in 1847, was a member of the Beth Israel Congregation.

In 1876 Beth Israel, Hartford's German-Jewish congregation, purchased land on Charter Oak Avenue and constructed the first building

intended for use as a Jewish synagogue in Connecticut. The architect was George Keller who also designed the Civil War Arch. In 1935 this old temple was sold and the congregation moved into a lovely new temple in West Hartford.

During the first quarter of the 20th century many other Jews began migrating into Hartford from Russia, Poland, Lithuania, the Ukraine, Hungary, Romania and Galacia. Because they all spoke different languages and had different national customs, they did not assimilate with the German Jews. Instead they banded together with their own countrymen, formed their own synagogues, and created their own self-help societies. By 1910 the newcomers outnumbered the German Jews five to one. Two years later Hartford's Jewish residents decided to merge all of their charitable organizations into one United Jewish Charities.

In 1978 the old temple on Charter Oak Avenue was placed on the National Register of Historic Places. That same year the Charter Oak Temple Restoration Association (COTRA) was formed to purchase and restore the building. Its goal is to make the old temple into an important cultural center for the entire community. It is significant that the Jewish community in Greater Hartford is now the tenth largest in the nation.

The handsome brownstone church shown at left, was constructed on the corner of Church and Ann streets by Hartford's Irish residents in 1851. It was designed by Patrick D. Keely of Brooklyn, New York. Keely later became the architect for Asylum Hill Congregational Church and the original Cathedral of St. Joseph. The old wooden church, Holy Trinity, burned to the ground soon after this new church was completed. According to local gossip, Holy Trinity ". . . was consigned to the flames by fate and Know-Nothing aid." The Know-Nothings were a violently anti-Catholic political faction in Connecticut in those days.

The first pastor of St. Patrick was a fiery man of Erin named Father John Brady. In 1854 he was removed from office for insubordination. Shortly after his discharge, he died. His devoted parishioners then insisted that he be buried in the shadow of the church he had built. His tomb may be seen just to the left of the main entrance of the sanctuary.

Father Brady's successor was Father James Hughes, described as a "pillar of strength to those who needed him and a critical antagonist to those who stepped out of line." Father Hughes fought both with and

ABOVE,
The Rev. Dr. James W.C.
Pennington.
RIGHT,
Isabella Beecher Hooker and her
husband John Hooker, 1891.
BELOW,
Harriet Beecher Stowe.
Oil on canvas, 1853.
FAR RIGHT,
Francis Gillette, another Nook
Farm Resident.

for his parishioners. He even bought stock in the New Haven Railroad for which many of his flock worked as day laborers. This enabled him to raise his voice at stockholders' meetings in support of his parishioners' economic interests. He also tended to their political interests by marching the men off to the polls every election day to vote a solid Democratic ticket.

After the passage of the Fugitive Slave Law in 1850, which required all runaway slaves to be returned to their masters, friendly sentiment in Hartford centered on the Rev. James W.C. Pennington. A fugitive from Maryland, Pennington had become pastor of the First Colored Congregational Church on Talcott Street in 1840. A popular preacher, he made three trips to Europe while serving the Hartford church. On his second trip, having already earned a wide reputation as a fighter for civil rights, he was awarded by the University of Heidelberg an honorary degree of Doctor of Divinity . . . the first time the university had conferred such an honor on a black man.

Fearing for the safety of Dr. Pennington, who was legally a fugitive slave, Hartford lawyer John Hooker formally purchased him from his Maryland master for $150. Before freeing his distinguished new "slave," Hooker kept the deed of sale for a few days. He explained that this was simply to experience the unique sensation of "owning" a doctor of divinity!

On June 5, 1851 Harriet Beecher Stowe's novel, *Uncle Tom's Cabin,* began to be serialized in a weekly abolitionist newspaper, the *National Era.* In 1852 it was published in book form . . . 37½ cents for the paperbound edition and $1.50 for the cloth-bound.

By 1853 almost 1.5 million English language copies of the book had been sold and many thousands more translated into foreign languages. This book was no doubt the most influential anti-slavery novel published prior to the Civil War. Mrs. Stowe's home on Forest Street is now an historic site and part of the Nook Farm complex.

Active in the abolitionist movement, Francis Gillette, father of the actor William Gillette, served in the U.S. Senate from 1854-1855. His home on Nook Farm was a "station" in the Underground Railroad that assisted runaway slaves en route to freedom in Canada.

ABOVE,
Potsdam Village, Hendricxsen Avenue.
BELOW,
"Der Hartforder Herald",
November 1890.
FAR RIGHT,
St. Lucia Festival at Emanuel Lutheran Church.
FAR RIGHT BOTTOM,
Henry Barnard.
Oil on canvas, 1886.

Immigrants to Hartford from England, Wales, Scotland, Holland, Germany and Scandanavia were looked upon with special favor by the native Yankees because they tended to be skilled, better educated, white and Protestant. In the 1850s when Sam Colt built a dike in the South Meadows to keep out the spring floods of the Connecticut River, he reinforced the dike by planting willow trees in the earthworks. The trees thrived. Soon Colt was troubled by the fact that willow shoots, valuable for making light furniture, were going to waste. Learning that the best makers of willow furniture were to be found in Potsdam, Germany, Colt offered to import the entire village if the villagers would agree to move to Hartford. He also promised to build them homes similar to those in their native village, to keep them well supplied with good, German beer, and to give them ample leisure time for playing their musical instruments. They agreed to his proposals. So Colt built a special factory for making willow furniture and constructed delightful, nearby homes for his new employees. Soon he was the leading manufacturer of willow furniture in America . . . and the Colt band was much enjoyed by all Hartford residents.

As newcomers from foreign lands settled in Hartford, many began publishing small, and often short-lived, newspapers in their native tongues. *Der Hartforder Herold* was first issued on May 5, 1883. Its headquarters were at 46 Market Street. No doubt it was preceded by earlier German weeklies as Germans began arriving in this city during the first half of the 19th century.

The old Swedish festival of St. Lucia still is celebrated every December 13 in Lutheran churches. A lovely young girl is chosen each year to impersonate St. Lucia. She is shown here, crowned with a coronet of candles, surrounded by her followers.

Because Scandinavian newcomers to Hartford tended to have an aptitude for skilled machine work, they were much in demand in places like Pratt & Whitney Machine Tool Company and other factories requiring precision work.

Born in Hartford in 1811, Barnard worked all his life trying to improve the public schools. In 1867 he became the first U.S. Commissioner of Education. Barnard died in his family home on Main Street in 1900. Barnard Park, formerly the South Green, is named in his honor. In 1966 the Henry Barnard House became a national landmark.

The public schools, which all the young were obliged to attend, were used by native Connecticut Yankees not only as educational institutions but as "melting pots" to turn the children of the foreign-born into proper Americans. When Roman Catholics objected to the Protestant emphasis of the public schools, they had to pay double in order to create their own parochial schools.

In 1855 anti-Catholic Know-Nothing William T. Minor was elected governor of Connecticut. One of his first acts was to pass a law mandating the dissolution of all military companies composed of foreign-born men. Actually only those companies manned by Irish Catholics were dissolved. Minor lost the next election, and in 1858 William A. Buckingham became the first Republican governor of the state. Throughout his campaign, Republicans were derided as "Negro Lovers and Irish Haters," Democrats as supporters of "Rum, Romanism and Slavery."

A solidly pro-Union, anti-slavery man, Buckingham was an ardent supporter of Abraham Lincoln. One of his first acts was to repeal the law dissolving military companies composed of the foreign-born. Then he recruited Connecticut's first all-Irish regiment, the 9th Connecticut Volunteers.

When the Civil War erupted, Connecticut was ready to fight. Before the war ended, almost 8,000 Irish clearly demonstrated that they were first-class American citizens. Many immigrant sons . . . Germans, Scots, Dutch, Scandinavians and others . . . also bravely spilled their blood for their adopted state and nation. Two regiments, the 29th and 30th, composed of 1,664 black Yankees, made an heroic contribution to final victory. Altogether, Connecticut sent into the Union Army over 54,000 men, 20,000 of whom became casualties.

Civil War Recruiting Poster.

Gideon Welles, Secretary of the Navy during the Civil War. Oil on canvas.

During and after the Civil War, Hartford's manufacturing economy boomed. This, of course, accelerated the influx of potential factory workers from out-of-state and from foreign shores. In 1871 the city's stature also was enhanced when Hartford was made the sole capital of Connecticut . . . an honor it had shared with New Haven up to this time. Gideon Welles, returning home after spending eight years in Washington, D.C. as President Lincoln's secretary of the Navy, was astonished by all the changes that had taken place in both the physical appearance and population of the city. "Hartford itself has greatly altered, I might say improved," he observed, "for it has been beautified and adorned by many magnificent buildings, and the population has increased. A new and different people seem to move in the streets. Few comparatively are known to me."

The number of "new and different people" migrating into Hartford before the turn of the 20th century peaked in 1882. Seven years later the Connecticut Bible Society and six students from the Hartford Theological Seminary, in a rather quixotic census, documented some of the radical changes in the ethnic backgrounds and religious affiliations of Hartford's residents: "The population of the city was found to be 48,179. The nationalities were as follows: American, 23,154, including 1,191 colored; Irish, 15,757; German, 3,060; English, 1,676; Scotch, 804; French, 798; Italian, 614; Swedish, 444; Danish, 367; Russian, 278; Polish, 65; Chinese, 31; Romanian and Bohemian, each 22. There are 85 others including these nationalities: Swiss, Norwegian, Hungarian, Spanish, Austrian, Portuguese, Greek, Welsh, Indian, Bulgarian, Hindu, Maltese, Hollander . . . There is one church to every 1,235 of population . . .

"The people were found to be divided according to religious belief as follows: Roman Catholic (80% Irish), 19,309; Congregational, 8,486; Episcopalian, 6,143; Methodist, 3,324; Baptist, 2,315; Lutheran, 1,458; Jews, 1,158; Universalist, 970; Presbyterian, 667; Unitarian, 276; Advent, 266; Spiritualist, 60; Catholic Apostolic, 36; no preference, 2,681 . . . There are in all 25,011 Protestants, 19,309 Roman Catholics and 1,158 Jews."

The seminarians also gathered the following significant bits of information about saloons and other evils. One has to keep in mind that prohibiting the sale and use of alcoholic beverages was a popular idea among many Protestants. "There are 222 licensed saloons in the city, and 388 women reported as prostitutes, besides a large number of doubtful cases. The returns from the jails show that out of 1,497 committed the last year as prisoners, only 7 were classed as 'strictly temperate.' At the town farm on June 23 there were 183 people, 98 men and 75 women, and 10 children. Of this number 137 were Irish."

From 1890 to 1925 a significant change took place in the national origin of many newcomers. Although some continued to arrive from Britain, Ireland and northern Europe, many more began migrating here from southern and eastern sectors of the Old World: Italy, France, Poland, Russia, the Ukraine, Austria, Lithuania, Hungary, Greece, Armenia. A few even came from the Middle and Far East, and an increasing number from French Canada. The majority were Roman Catholics. The number of blacks in the city continued to be around 3 percent of the total population.

Hartford's three major "ports-of-entry" for new immigrants were centered on Front and Market streets, Sheldon Street and Charter Oak Avenue, and Capitol Avenue and Park Street. In these neighborhoods newcomers could seek and find, sometimes at a local bar, a potential friend. The wiser and more fortunate would have someone waiting to greet them. There was much correspondence back and forth between friends and relatives in the "old country" and immigrants already living here who had "learned the ropes" about surviving in the city. It was not unusual for young men to board with families that had come from their native villages. Then, after finding a job, the men would send for their wives and children and set up housekeeping in an available tenement. Because the factories in which most found employment tended to be located in these three parts of the city, the men could easily walk to work.

Churches and synagogues, the nuclei of each small neighborhood, played a key role in enabling newcomers to become stable, productive citizens. Catholics, Jews and Protestants could immediately contact religious institutions that suited their particular preferences. Then they tended to join forces with fellow countrymen to create new places of worship in which their own language was spoken and native customs and traditions observed. This was essential to their becoming rooted in the city.

New immigrants usually were poor, lonely, frightened, disorganized and woefully lacking in self-esteem. The religious institutions became their extended families, their support groups. Within the church or synagogue they could find both protection and self-respect . . . all humans being equal in the sight of God. The priests, ministers and rabbis also taught them how to behave like children of God by stressing Biblical rules of conduct, a close-knit family life and a rigorous work ethic.

French Social Club, Park Street, 1986.

Numerous small fraternal clubs and societies were formed within the synagogues and churches . . . clubs like B'nai B'rith (Brothers of the Covenant); St. Patrick's Benevolent Society; St. John's Sick and Burial Society; a variety of sisterhoods; political, athletic and musical clubs and marching bands . . . all related to the particular ethnic heritage of each group. By joining together they bolstered one another's spirits, helped one another to find jobs, and took care of one another in time of trouble.

Ethnic "ghettos" also were political power bases. Religious leaders often gave their parishioners astute political advice and marched them off to the polls on election day. In this way the newcomers gradually gained control of City Hall . . . a city-wide political power base from which to bargain with those who controlled the financial and business enterprises in Hartford. Thus the poor were empowered spiritually, economically and politically. As a result, in two or three generations, many rose to commanding positions of leadership in the wider community.

Hartford's business and political leaders and their wives created settlement houses and special health, recreational and educational programs to assist the new immigrants coming into the city. Mrs. Samuel Colt was a leader in the settlement house movement. Later the Junior League of Hartford played an important part in bringing new or improved services to the less fortunate members of the community. In 1924 the Hartford Community Chest, now the United Way of the Capital Area, was created in order to bring properly coordinated, professional social services to those in need.

In 1854 the Missionary Society of Christ Church (Episcopal) constructed this curious little brownstone building on 125 Market Street to minister to new immigrants from Germany who were beginning to settle in this section of the city. Three years later the building was officially named St. Paul's Church. In 1880 the German Lutherans purchased the building from the Episcopalians and renamed it Church of the Reformation.

By 1889 this part of Hartford was becoming heavily Italian, and the Germans were moving south toward Charter Oak Avenue. There they purchased a new church and, in 1898, sold their old one to the Italians who renamed it St. Anthony. They used the building first as a church, then as a recreation center . . . Casa Maria . . . after they had built a new church on Talcott Street.

In the 1950s, when plans were being made to construct Constitution Plaza, almost all the buildings in this area, with the exception of Casa Maria, were demolished. In 1958 St. Anthony merged with St. Patrick Church on the corner of Church and Ann streets. Today this durable little brownstone structure is owned by the Roman Catholic Diocese of Hartford.

During the first quarter of the 20th century Italians outnumbered all other newcomers to Hartford. Some went to work in local factories, others became stonemasons, bricklayers, shoemakers, bakers, and proprietors of "mom and pop" restaurants. Others took up picks and shovels as day laborers to build the new highways needed for the recently-invented automobile. Italian names still are dominant in the heavy construction business. Today, however, many are employers owning huge earth-moving equipment.

In this land of opportunity an Italian who earned his family's living as a scissor grinder in one of the large insurance companies had the satisfaction of seeing his son become a junior executive in that same company.

A large majority of the progeny of immigrants to Hartford from foreign lands made similar progress up the economic and political ladder to success by standing on the shoulders of their industrious parents.

Before urban renewal, peddlers with pushcarts used to line city streets hawking a glorious variety of dry goods and foods. Vendors of milk, eggs, vegetables, fruits, chickens and other perishables sold leftover produce from their wagons at half price before returning to their farms.

This portion of the Park River now is covered by the Conland-Whitehead connector leading to I-91. The tenements on the right

fronted on Sheldon Street. This area used to be the heart of the old Polish neighborhood. Today the Polish National Home, Sts. Cyril & Methodius Church on Governor Street and the statue of Count Casimir Pulaski that fronts on Main Street are reminders of this bygone era.

Until World War I women never worked as machine operators and inspectors in Hartford's factories. However, with so many men off on the fighting fronts, factory owners began experiencing an acute labor shortage. They placed large ads in newspapers and on outdoor billboards proclaiming: "MAKING MUNITIONS IS A WOMAN'S JOB."

ABOVE,
Sts. Cyril and Methodius Church
(Polish; built 1917), 1986.

ABOVE RIGHT,
Polish National Home, Capitol
Avenue, c. 1970.

RIGHT,
World War I Poster.

The president of the Allen Manufacturing Company on Sheldon Street even began stopping sturdy looking women in the neighborhood and urging them to come to work in his factory. When they declined because they had young children, he rented a nearby saloon, tore out the bar, placed a sandbox in the store-front window where it could be clearly visible, filled the place with attractive toys, and hired a couple of nurses to care for the young. Then he personally brought the mothers to see his improvised day care center. Many were newcomers from Poland and still unable to speak English. But they understood what they saw, brought in their children, and went to work for Allen.

Other manufacturers in the area copied Allen's example. As added attractions they installed new rest rooms and neat cafeterias and put special safety devices on the machines. Hartford's employers were astonished by the women's skill and their ability to produce as much as the men.

The introduction of females into factories as machine operators and inspectors was a revolutionary and permanent change in their economic status. An equally revolutionary change in their political status occurred in 1920 when women finally won the right to vote.

Women factory workers, c. 1895.

Isabella Beecher Hooker, a resident of Forest Street and wife of John Hooker, became the first president of the Connecticut Woman Suffrage Association in 1869. She continued in office until 1905 when she was succeeded by another Hartford resident, Annie Elliot Trumbull. Miss Trumbull, a very conservative lady, was rather abruptly replaced by some younger women in the city who aspired to run a more vigorous campaign to win the vote. So in 1910, Mrs. Thomas N. Hepburn (Katharine Houghton Hepburn) became the third president of the C.W.S.A.

The new leaders of the Association immediately opened up an office on Pratt Street from which they distributed quantities of suffrage literature. The suffragettes held numerous parades demanding the vote and lobbied regularly at both the state and national capitols. On a number of occasions they invited Emmeline Pankhurst, the radical English suffragette, to speak at the Parsons Theater in Hartford. At least three times a week the flamboyant activities of the suffragettes made news on the front pages of the *Hartford Courant*, which opposed them, and the *Hartford Times*, which supported them.

In 1917 Mrs. Hepburn resigned as president of the C.W.S.A. to join Alice Paul's Woman's Party that was seeking not only the vote but an Equal Rights Amendment. She was succeeded by Katharine Luddington of Old Lyme. In September of 1920 Connecticut had the dishonor of becoming the last state to ratify the 19th Amendment to the U.S. Constitution that finally gave women the franchise.

ABOVE,
Katharine Houghton Hepburn, third president of the C.W.S.A. and the four oldest of her six children.

RIGHT,
Suffrage headquarters on Pratt Street.

See Appendices for Population Charts.

Between 1900 and 1930 the number of foreign-born and/or their children and grandchildren almost doubled in the city of Hartford. During that same period of time, especially after World War I, the old Yankees began moving out into the suburbs of the Capitol Region.

Hartford fared better than most cities during the Great Depression because the insurance companies made a major effort to keep their employees in their jobs.

RIGHT,
Health Clinic for poor children.
BELOW RIGHT,
Newcomers learning English in night school.

76

Mother with five soldier sons.

This proud mother with her five sons who served their country in World War II represents every American mother who made a similar sacrifice.

Most of Hartford's returning veterans had little desire to go back to their old ethnic neighborhoods. The comprehensive G.I. Bill of Rights was a great boon because it offered them a gamut of educational opportunities as well as guaranteed loans for home mortgages. More education qualified them for all kinds of better jobs, and small down payments enabled them to purchase their own homes either in Hartford or in the suburbs.

Many, but not all, when they moved out of the city settled down near others from their old neighborhoods. One old Italian was not completely happy with suburban living. He missed his Front Street home in "Little Italy." "In the old days," he said, "you could walk out on the street any hour of the day and meet friends. Now you have to call them up on the telephone and make an appointment."

After World War I and during World War II many southern blacks and Jamaicans migrated into Hartford, attracted by the demand for both agricultural and industrial labor. Many settled in the north end of the city. Unfortunately friction between black and white residents developed. So the governor appointed a state-wide Interracial Commission chaired by the Rt. Rev. Walter H. Gray, Suffragan Bishop of the Episcopal Diocese of Connecticut.

Early in 1943 the Rev. Dr. John C. Jackson, pastor of Hartford's Union Baptist Church, while traveling on a train through Alabama, was attacked and cruelly beaten by two white men as he passed through a coach reserved for whites to join some friends. While the incident was widely reported in the nation's press, Dr. Jackson was unable to obtain any satisfaction from the U.S. Justice Department.

Local indignation, however, was intense as Dr. Jackson was much admired in Hartford. Bishop Gray immediately came to his assistance. Then, on June 29 of that year, the Connecticut Civil Rights Commission was created . . . the first in the nation. Bishop Gray became chairman of the new Commission and Dr. Jackson a member.

By 1970 forty-five percent of Hartford's school children were black. So, for the first time, Hartford's black residents were sufficiently numerous to exercise some real political "clout." This they did in 1981 when Thirman L. Milner became mayor . . . the first black mayor to be elected in New England.

Blacks also began to move ahead economically. When the Urban League, financed by Hartford's business community, was brought to the city in 1964, qualified blacks finally were able to find suitable employment despite racial prejudices. As a result, Hartford began to develop a sizable black middle class, many of whom now have moved to the suburbs.

As with other ethnic groups, local churches, self-help clubs and civil rights organizations have played important roles in promoting the upward mobility of Hartford's black citizens. The Prince Hall Masons, sororities, fraternities, and the NAACP are among many that have made important contributions to the welfare of their constituents.

During the 1980s the Greater Hartford Chamber of Commerce, the city and the state established a wide assortment of education and training programs to assist less qualified blacks, Hispanics and other minorities to become employable. This is an ongoing effort that involves close cooperation between job-makers, schools, social services, churches and individual families.

Between 1973 and 1983 the number of black students in the city's elementary schools *decreased* from 46.8 percent to 42.1 percent . . . and in the high schools increased only slightly from 48.9 percent to 49.5 percent. However, between 1975 and 1985 the total number of black students in Hartford's schools *decreased* by 10 percent. It is indicative of the upward and outward mobility of Hartford's former black residents that the number of minority students in the city's contiguous suburb of Bloomfield by 1985 had risen to 65 percent of the students enrolled in that school system.

Hispanics from Puerto Rico, Cuba, Central and South America have been migrating into Hartford since the 1940s. They have settled chiefly in the vicinity of Park Street in the South End and Clay Hill in the North End. The better educated have been rapidly assimilated into the wider community. Those lacking skills and education have found employment in a variety of entry-level jobs or have taken advantage of the city's special education and training programs. Like the newcomers of yesteryear, they have been greatly assisted by their churches . . . Roman Catholic, Protestant and Pentacostal. Clubs like La Casa de Puerto Rico and the Spanish-American Businessmen's Association also have helped them to help themselves.

TOP
Thirman L. Milner.
ABOVE,
In 1979 Antonio Gonzalez became the first Hispanic to be popularly elected to Hartford's City Council.
RIGHT,
The annual Park Street festival is enjoyed by many.

Today about 20 percent of Hartford's residents are Hispanic. Many now own their own homes and businesses. In 1983 Hartford school officials revealed the astonishing fact that, during the past 10 years, the number of Hispanic youngsters in the city's elementary schools increased from 25.8 percent to 42.6 percent . . . and the number in the high schools from 18.3 percent to 36.1 percent. This same year Hispanics also demonstrated their growing political strength by electing Nancy Melendez to Hartford's City Council.

Newcomers from a variety of foreign lands, even the Orient, are now migrating into Hartford (see Appendix). Despite obvious language barriers, most Asians are doing very well economically thanks to their emphasis on the traditional "keys" to upward mobility . . . family cohesiveness, education and a strong work ethic.

Perhaps the best reminders of Hartford's past and indicators of its future are the city's many religious institutions, old and new, that highlight Hartford's ethnic and religious diversity. In 350 years Hartford indeed has developed from being an exclusive Puritan settlement into one of the most inclusive cities in the world today.

TOP,
*Holy Trinity Church
(Lithuanian; built 1927),
Capitol Avenue, 1986.*
ABOVE,
*All Saints Russian Orthodox
Church (built 1964),
Scarborough Street, c. 1970.*
TOP RIGHT,
*St. George Armenian Apostolic
Church (built 1953), White
Street, 1986.*
BELOW RIGHT,
*St. George Greek Orthodox
Church (built 1968), Fairfield
Avenue, 1986.*

RIGHT,
*St. Ann's Church (French; built
1926) Park Street, 1986.*
BELOW,
*Our Lady of Fatima Church
(Portuguese; built 1986), 1986.*

This parade of Connecticut Bicycle Club velocipedes took place in September 1885, when bicycling was a popular sport for young men who dared to mount the two-wheelers.

Then and Now

The only building still surviving between Pearl and Gold on the west side of Main Street is the Center Congregational Church.

Looking west in 1834, only 15 years after Society for Savings was founded.

Completely restored, Hartford's oldest landmark seems to sit primly on an island of repose amid a sea of new downtown development.

During the 1860s it was the horsecar.

Now the sleek motor bus.

The original location of the Asylum for Deaf and Dumb Persons,
opened in 1817, where now are located . . .

Headquarters of the Hartford Insurance Group, founded in 1810 as the Hartford Fire Insurance Company. Frances Wadsworth's sculpture honors Thomas Hopkins Gallaudet, Mason Fitch Cogswell and Laurent Clerc, founders of the country's oldest school for the deaf.

A reservoir on this hill provided the city of Hartford drinking water, raised by a Woodruff & Beach pump from the Connecticut River, from 1854 to 1876. This view of the reservoir looks south toward the Capitol.

As does the modern one, with the original Hartford Fire building
(1921) in the right foreground.

Church spires dominated the skyline around 1837.

Today almost lost amid surrounding offices and stores.

Looking south from the corner of Church Street at the head of which is the Episcopal Cathedral.

Today only the Cathedral looks the same.

The Old Stone Bridge (1834) on Main Street crossed the Park River, which flowed past Hartford tenements and emptied into the Connecticut at Dutch Point.

Hartford's Public Library (1957) sits east of the bridge over the
Whitehead connector to I-91, under which the Park River still flows.

In 1890 was a decrepit "red light" district, but Emily Holcombe, the zealous local regent of the D.A.R., led a crusade to clean it up and also to improve the Ancient Burying Ground.

Today it is a major thoroughfare between Trumbull and Main streets.

When Union Station was erected in 1849, the tracks ran at ground level across Asylum Street.

The tracks were elevated in 1889 and the entire structure radically redesigned. The brownstone station is again undergoing renovation into a transportation center.

On the southwest side of Trumbull Street Greater Hartford's oldest
extant printing establishment, Case, Lockwood & Co. (now
Connecticut Printers in Bloomfield) started in 1836, when Hartford
was a major publishing center. The building (1793) was originally the
city jail.

It was demolished in the 1960s to make way for Southern New England Telephone Company's 10-story Communications Center. Thus, the development of the information revolution from the printed to the spoken word can, in Hartford anyway, be said to have occurred on one site.

The Allyn House, on the northwest corner of Asylum and Trumbull Streets, opened in 1857 and was the city's leading hostelry in the last decades of the 19th century.

The Civic Center, opened in 1975, is the nucleus of post-industrial Hartford's successful revival.

The opening of Parsons Theater on the corner of Central Row and
Prospect Street in 1896 was a major event in Hartford's theatrical life.
It was torn down in 1936 to make way for . . .

The headquarters of the Hartford Steam Boiler Inspection and Insurance Company, which in 1983 moved into one of the city's newest skyscrapers at One State Street and sold this corner to The Travelers Insurance Companies.

In the early 20th century, Charles Street, along with Front and Market streets, was part of a vibrant neighborhood near the river where the earliest immigrants settled.

In the 1960s the tenements, stores, saloons and pushcarts disappeared as the concrete grandeur of Constitution Plaza, Hartford's first post-war urban renewal project, took shape.

For 300 years the city had direct access to its riverfront, as this view of
State Street, looking east from the Old State House during a flood
of 1870, clearly shows.

Construction of the 45-foot high dike wiped out the entire dock area in 1941, and 10 years later the interstate highway separated the people of Hartford even farther from the Connecticut River.

Capitol Avenue was the center of Hartford's metal-working industries for some 75 years, where pioneering companies like Robbins & Lawrence, Weed Sewing Machine, Pope Manufacturing, Pratt & Whitney (shown here) and Underwood Typewriter refined Eli Whitney's system of mass production.

Today, reflecting the domination of financial services in Hartford's economy—and the decline of manufacturing—Aetna Life & Casualty has converted the old factory buildings into offices.

Began as the result of a tragic accident—the explosion of the Fales &
Gray Car Works which killed 21 and injured 50. Its first patient was
admitted in 1860.

The hospital we see today was completed in 1948, the seventh largest in the United States.

From downtown to Woodland Street, where the horse car terminated, Farmington Avenue was graced by many fine homes, such as Francis B. Cooley's . . .

Now the location for Aetna Life & Casualty, the largest office building in the colonial style anywhere, built in 1931.

Across the street from the Aetna the massive Portland brownstone Cathedral of St. Joseph was consecrated in 1892 and destroyed by fire in 1956.

Six years later it was replaced by this vast sanctuary, which features a white marble altar, a gigantic ceramic mural of Christ in Glory, and French stained-glass windows.

Travelers Insurance has always been in the center of the city since its founding in 1863.

The Tower Square complex, leading to the main entrance, was
completed at the time of its 100th anniversary.

The Main Street home of Jeremiah Wadsworth, Hartford's wealthiest merchant before and after the Revolution, welcomed many famous visitors like George Washington and General Lafayette.

In 1842 when his son Daniel commissioned the building of the Atheneum, the Wadsworth mansion was relocated to Buckingham Street to clear the site for the Wadsworth Atheneum, the country's oldest public art museum.

Hartford's high-class residential district after the Civil War may have inspired Mark Twain's observation, when he first visited the city in 1868, that "of all the beautiful towns it has been my fortune to see, this is the chief. . . ."

Today, presided over by the statue of Columbus (dedicated in 1926), the area consists mainly of state government offices and courts.

Trinity College, founded as Washington College in 1823, had to move from its original site in 1872 to make way for . . .

The State Capitol, recently cleaned and renovated in celebration of its 100th anniversary.

Union Settlement House,
founded in 1872 to assist
Hartford's poorest residents.

Hartford Cares . . .

From the earliest days the enthusiasm of Hartford's leaders for practical philanthropy was founded on their Puritan heritage. Most of them were merchants, businessmen or hard-working farmers who aspired to be economically successful. But they also were devoted to the welfare of the entire community, taking seriously the Biblical admonition ". . . from everyone to whom much has been given, much shall be required. . . ." Diligence in one's calling, thrift and a concern for the unfortunate were among the most highly regarded virtues of the founders, and they persevered during the long process of secularizaton, as Puritans changed to Yankees.

Those in Connecticut who acquired wealth during the early days of the republic were almost certain to be faithful Congregationalists, staunch Federalists (or conservatives) and members of the Standing Order—the power structure of that period. Even more to the point, those engaging in philanthropy were in many instances descended from clergymen. Religion supplied the spiritual motivation and vision, while business experience made them no-nonsense do-gooders. And the concentration of wealth in Hartford because of its economic diversity provided the wherewithal to share it for the common good.

Daniel Wadsworth, son of Jeremiah and descendant of a first settler, might well be called Connecticut's first full-time philanthropist. In delicate health most of his life, having almost no formal schooling and blessed with a large inheritance, he could not help but become the first of his generation who found it unnecessary to earn his own living. In his father's mansion on Main Street he was exposed to distinguished visitors like General Washington and the Count de Rochambeau; as a youth of 12 he accompanied his father to Paris, where his lifelong interest in art was aroused. Growing up a shy, yet conscientious man, he married in 1794 Faith Trumbull, the daughter of Governor Jonathan Trumbull Jr. and niece of the painter John Trumbull. Later Daniel built a rustic villa and tower on the top of Talcott Mountain, where he loved to retreat and to paint landscapes. The young Wadsworths were enthusiastic patrons of the arts. Another Hartfordite, Thomas Cole, became one of the first great American landscape painters through the Wadsworths' support.

Wadsworth's elegant yellow coach and conspicuous attire, consisting of several capes of differing lengths and colors, fascinated his fellow citizens, who in 1817 numbered only 6,000. It was a time of momentous political and economic change, as the old Federalist party and the Standing Order of ministers and merchants which had dominated every aspect of life for so long saw their power crumble. The following year the Republican-Tolerationists under Oliver Wolcott Jr. won overwhelmingly in the state elections and set about to disestablish the Congregational church, guarantee religious freedom and encourage industrial growth.

Daniel, now in his 40s, eschewing politics, began to take a deep interest in making Hartford a better place in which to live. The impetus was the founding, in 1817, of the Connecticut Asylum for the Education and Instruction of Deaf and Dumb Persons, the first institution in America devoted to the handicapped. Dr. Mason F. Cogswell, one of the three founders and a friend of Daniel's since his childhood, per-

ABOVE,
Daniel Wadsworth.
Oil on canvas.
BELOW,
Asylum for Deaf and Dumb
Persons.
Engraving.

suaded the latter to lend financial support. Two years later Wadsworth helped to establish the state's first mutual savings bank—to encourage thrift among newcomers to Hartford—and agreed to serve as president of the Society for Savings.

Three years later he responded generously to the eloquent plea of Dr. Eli Todd of Hartford for a mental hospital, founded as the Hartford Retreat, the oldest hospital in Connecticut and the third oldest in the United States. In 1833 Daniel helped to organize the Hartford Orphan Asylum, now called Children's Services of Connecticut.* However, his greatest philanthropy, conceived by himself, was still to come. Like the Asylum and the Retreat, it was an innovation for the country. In 1841 he broached the idea of erecting a public art museum and offered to donate the land—where his father's house stood—on condition that an association be formed. The sum of $20,000 was promptly subscribed, $6,500 by Daniel himself. The three-wing Gothic structure was completed in 1844 at a cost of $35,000. The Wadsworth home was moved to Buckingham Street. With his knowledge of art, Daniel bought paintings for the Wadsworth Atheneum and persuaded others to do the same. At its opening five historical scenes of the Revolution by John Trumbull were on display, and in his will the famous painter bequeathed five more of his works to the museum. The Atheneum also housed The Connecticut Historical Society (1825) and the Young Men's Institute (1838), later the Hartford Public Library. Four years later, at the age of 77, Daniel Wadsworth died, having sponsored every important charitable cause of his day.

Another well-to-do resident was soon inspired to emulate Wadsworth's selfless generosity. Born in England, uncle to the Collins brothers who started the axe and machete factory along the Farmington River in Canton, David Watkinson finally settled in Hartford, where he amassed a fortune as a merchant engaged in the West Indies trade and later in hardware. Childless, he left at his death in 1857 an estate said to be the largest ever probated in the city up to that time. (Five years later Colonel Samuel Colt's demise at the age of 47 resulted in a much bigger estate, none of which went to charity.) Watkinson's will provided, among other bequests, $100,000 to establish "a free reference library"

*Actually, the first institution for the protection of minors was the Hartford Female Beneficent Society, organized in 1809, from which the orphanage grew.

as part of the Wadsworth Atheneum, $40,000 for the new Hartford Hospital and a substantial sum for the Hartford Orphan Society. In addition, he set aside $20,000 in cash and 10 acres of land valued at $40,000 for what he called "a juvenile asylum for neglected and abandoned children," the largest bequest made to a secondary school until then.

To develop plans for the school Watkinson relied entirely upon his good friend Henry Barnard, who advised him to model it after similar institutions already existing in France and Germany and described by the great educator in his book, *National Education In Europe*. The one near Hamburg, established in 1833, aimed to reclaim "abandoned children of the very lowest class . . . from habits of idleness, vagrancy and crime by making them feel the blessing of a Christian and domestic life, and the pleasure of earning their own bread . . . ." Watkinson visualized the enrollees as being orphans between the ages of 6 and 21 in danger of delinquency. Five years after his death, in 1862, the General Assem-

bly granted a charter for the "Juvenile Asylum & Farm School for Orphan Boys," but 18 more years were to pass before it opened.

In fact, without the firm hand of Hartford's most prominent, powerful and richest aristocrat after Daniel Wadsworth, Watkinson School might never have been developed. He was Francis Goodwin, who succeeded to the crown of philanthropy worn by the Wadsworths for two generations. Like them, Goodwin's family was descended from one of the original settlers. They were adept at acquiring valuable real estate and seizing new opportunities. Jonathan and James Goodwin, representing the fourth and fifth generations, ran a popular inn on the Albany Turnpike one mile west of the city. James Jr., while still a minor, acquired ownership of the profitable stage line running east from Hartford, operating 40 coaches and stabling 400 horses. Anticipating that the "iron horse" would soon make stagecoaches obsolete, he gradually disposed of his business and invested in the Hartford and New Haven Railroad.

The unlimited horizon of insurance also attracted him, and in 1846 he led a group of businessmen who obtained a charter for the first mutual life insurance company. Except for a four-year period James Goodwin Jr. ran Connecticut Mutual for three decades until his death in 1878. He also married well, taking as his bride Lucy Morgan, sister of Junius S. Morgan, who bore him seven children.

Real estate, however, continued to be the family's major interest. Major James Jr. was Hartford's largest individual taxpayer, as was his son, the Rev. Francis Goodwin. Born like Daniel Wadsworth with the proverbial silver spoon in his mouth, Francis tried a business career but finally gave in to his mother's plea to enter the ministry of the Episcopal church. After 12 years in the pulpit, his father's death prompted him to withdraw from the ministry and, in association with his older brother, to devote all his time to the family's business interests and community affairs. For many years he headed the board of the Wadsworth Atheneum, persuading his cousin J.P. Morgan to build the Morgan Memorial wing, and was also involved with Trinity College, the Hartford Retreat and Watkinson Library.

But his consuming passion was to create a city-wide park system, extending the central park conceived by the liberal Congregational preacher, Horace Bushnell. Bushnell deplored the conditions surrounding the Park River which flowed through the city and emptied into the Connecticut. It had become a smelly, unsightly industrial slum—the first view of Hartford that railroad passengers saw as trains rounded the sharp bend from the south. After a hard struggle he convinced the city fathers to turn the slum into a central park, and the voters approved the purchase of the land in January 1854. The 37-acre area became the country's oldest municipal park. Three days before Bushnell's death in 1876 it was named in his honor.

One admirer said Francis Goodwin "boxed the compass of the city with beauty," and it all happened within the space of 14 months. On trips abroad he had been impressed by the natural beauty of England's lovely rolling estates and public parks; he knew too about the seven-mile chain of parks called the "Emerald Necklace" outside of Boston. During the 1870s, park systems in other cities like Brooklyn and even national parks like Yellowstone were coming into vogue. Why, Goodwin pondered, couldn't Hartford have a ring of parks around its perim-

ABOVE,
Rev. Francis Goodwin.
RIGHT,
Dr. Horace Bushnell.
Oil on canvas, c. 1840.

eter connected someday by parkways encircling the city?

What kind of man was this missionary in his own backyard? Mild and unassuming, a lover of good food; a patriarch to his devoted wife and eight children; an old-fashioned Puritan in his heritage; a hale and hearty frame—despite a supposedly weak heart—which supported him for 84 years; a man who never learned to play, grew restless and weary on his holidays at his summer home in Fenwick; and who gave generously of his time and fortune for more than 50 years. Though idealistic, his ventures were shrewdly conducted; his business inheritance combined with his ministerial experience made him the perfect social entrepreneur.

In 1880, the year Watkinson School took in its first pupils, Goodwin joined the Board of Park Commissioners and dominated it for the next 30 years. Until the Park Board became virtually independent of the city government in 1895, he made little headway; then, quickly, all of the components of his grand scheme fell into place. He first persuaded his cousin, a childless wholesale grocer, Henry Keney, to leave his entire fortune in trust for the acquisition of some 600 acres of farmland and woodlot in the north part of the city to create Keney Park. In the summer of that same year, 1894, he convinced another wealthy citizen, also childless—Charles M. Pond—to donate his land spanning the borders of Hartford and West Hartford as a garden park in memory of his wife Elizabeth. In November Colonel Albert Pope, head of Hartford's largest factory and the country's leading producer of bicycles, responded to Goodwin's plea for a park in the southwest section, contributing 90 acres and $100,000 for maintenance.

In the meantime Goodwin had received a visit from the city's reigning dowager, who controlled a mile square of the South Meadows, bounded by her palatial home, Armsmear, on the west and the Connecticut River on the east. As the daughter of an Episcopal minister and Colonel Colt's widow, Elizabeth Jarvis Colt was revered as a benefactress without peer. She helped to found the Union for Home Work (1872)—Hartford's first settlement house—and was its president for 20 years. She too wanted to help Goodwin and agreed to provide in her will for a gift to the city of around 100 acres. Before her death in 1905 she commissioned the elaborate memorial to the inventor of the revolver that marks the entrance to Colt Park.

Bushnell Park, 1903.

Statue of Samuel Colt in Colt Park, c. 1970.

Early in 1895, using bond proceeds, the Park Board acquired 80 acres in the North End along the riverfront and 200 acres in the South End. Riverside Park was to be a demonstration of Goodwin's sincere belief that parks should exist for everyone's benefit, not merely as a rendezvous for well-to-do folk cavorting in fancy carriages. The site was accessible to the crowded tenements of the east side. Much to his embarrassment, the South End park was named for Goodwin in 1901. The architectural firm of Hartford–born Frederick L. Olmsted, designed both of them as well as Pope Park. Elizabeth Park was laid out by Theodore Wirth, who became superintendent of Hartford's parks in March 1896; its central attraction is still the oldest municipal rose garden with its 900 varieties and more than 14,000 bushes.

Francis Goodwin's vision—six parks covering 1,000 acres—was now a reality, and he survived another quarter of a century to see them flower. To the very day of his death in 1923 he continued to work, manipulate and bestow. His estate was valued at $6.6 million, another record, and the *Courant* bemoaned the loss of "our best citizen."

Charles A. Goodwin, one of Francis' four sons, carried on the Goodwin quest for civic betterment, but his approach was political rather than philanthropic, his goal a powerful regional agency to store and deliver water. Watching the city and its suburbs burgeon, he realized the acute need for an ample water supply, one that must be met at least a decade in advance. And he decided that only some kind of representative inter-town body could perform the service without compromising the jealously-guarded, inward-looking autonomy of individual towns. It was a daring, almost unprecedented concept for which he had to struggle year after year during the 1920s in the Legislature, against charges of being a wild-eyed visionary, if not a dangerous socialist, trying to create a super-government that would destroy local rule.

Success finally came in 1929 when the Legislature passed a bill authorizing the Metropolitan District and a referendum in the fall won voter approval in five towns. Only West Hartford opposed it. Goodwin became the District's first chairman and served continuously for the next 20 years.

Today the Metropolitan District's system covers more than 150 square miles, providing water of superior quality and treating the sewage discharged by some 600,000 residents in nine towns and parts of two more. When Charles Goodwin died in 1954, the *Courant* editorialized: "Generations yet unborn will owe much to (him) . . . for he was the father of the Metropolitan District . . . Here was a life, begun and ended in Hartford, that sums up much that has been good in Hartford and New England."

MDC Headquarters (left) and Bushnell Tower (right), 1984.

Other charitable endeavors should be mentioned. Hartford's Y.M.C.A., founded in 1852, is the second oldest in the country. The Y.W.C.A. began 15 years later. Hartford was late in setting up its first general hospital. The explosion of a factory boiler in March 1854, killing 21 persons and injuring some 50 more, resulted in a public outcry that led within weeks to the chartering of the Hartford Hospital. The city's two other hospitals, St. Francis and Mount Sinai, were founded, respectively, in 1898 and 1923.

Social service agencies multiplied late in the 19th century, such as the Woman's Aid Society (1878) "for the reformation of fallen women," the Connecticut Humane Society (1881) and the Open Hearth Mission (1884) for homeless men. A census taken by the Connecticut Bible Society in 1889 showed 18 societies and funds disbursing charity in Hartford. All of the 39 churches were doing some kind of relief work in addition to seven institutions. The report concluded with a statement as apt today as it must have been then:

> "There are then among us no less than 64 public charitable agencies, besides a large number of more private associations and a multitude of personal givers, all working independently and without common understanding or general cooperation. A clearing house would seem to be a necessity, both to prevent fraud and make intelligent application of relief possible."

Later came the Visiting Nurse Association (1901), the Charter Oak Council of the Boy Scouts of America (1914), the Greater Hartford Girl Scouts (1920) and the Junior League (1921).

Inevitably, as the city grew, philanthropy became more institutionalized. Especially after the Great Depression and the introduction of federal and state welfare programs, good works no longer depended solely on churches or individual movers and shakers like the Wadsworths and Goodwins. Yet modern examples of generous family philanthropy have been set by such well-known business leaders as Beatrice Auerbach, Clayton Gengras and Robert C. Knox, whose capital gifts have benefited scores of institutions like St. Joseph College, Science Center of Connecticut, Institute for Living, University of Hartford, the Y.M.C.A. and the Boys' Club. Mr. Knox's sister Betty, a Hartford councilwoman, established in her will the Knox Foundation, best known for the mini-parks around the city and the carousel in Bushnell Park.

Fund-raising for a variety of social purposes and the distribution of grants by corporations and foundations are still major activities. In fact, Hartford has a well-earned national reputation for being a caring city. As in the past, local businessmen and women are actively involved with City Hall and the Board of Education in ameliorating the transition from industrial to high technology and service through intensive job recruitment and training programs. At the forefront of this effort is the Greater Hartford Chamber of Commerce. The 10 largest companies all have departments of community affairs that together invest millions of dollars in a multitude of projects. Additional support is provided by several local foundations. Organized in 1925, the Hartford Foundation for Public Giving is the seventh largest public foundation in the United States, with accumulated assets of nearly $100 million. Between 1936 and 1985 it distributed $49 million to education, hospitals, social service agencies, and the arts.

An 1889 architect's conception of proposed Y.M.C.A. building.

Founding Dates of Hartford Charitable Institutions

1792	Charitable Society in Hartford
1792	Connecticut Society for the Promotion of Freedom
1809	Hartford Female Beneficent Society
1816	Hartford Evangelical Tract Society
1817	American Asylum for the Deaf
1818	Hartford Sunday School Society
1822	Hartford Retreat for the Insane
1824	Washington College (now Trinity College)
1825	The Connecticut Historical Society
1842	Wadsworth Atheneum
1852	Y.M.C.A.
1854	Hartford Hospital
1847	Widow's Society
1859	Hartford City Missionary Society
1867	Y.W.C.A.
1872	Union for Home Work
1878	Woman's Aid Society
1880	Good Will Club; Watkinson School
1881	Connecticut Humane Society
1884	Open Hearth Mission
1898	St. Francis Hospital
1901	Visiting Nurse Association
1905	Mitchell House
1914	Boy Scouts
1920	Girl Scouts
1921	Junior League of Hartford
1923	Mount Sinai Hospital
1925	Hartford Foundation for Public Giving
1971	Greater Hartford Arts Council

8

Literary Hartford

In the decade after the American Revolution a diverse group of Connecticut intellectuals banded together in a literary circle that centered in Hartford, the first of its kind in the new nation and the first to concentrate on truly American themes. Patriotic satirists, the Hartford Wits were mostly Yale graduates. Theodore Dwight and John Trumbull were lawyers, Lemuel Hopkins a physician; Richard Alsop of Middletown was part owner of a Hartford bookstore; Joel Barlow and Elisha Babcock published the *American Mercury;* and David Humphreys of Derby, then in his 30s, would excel as an ambassador and manufacturer as well as a playwright and biographer of Israel Putnam. Their patron was Jeremiah Wadsworth.

The Wits wrote in verse which usually appeared originally in the *Courant* or *Mercury* and long epics that are seldom read today. Meeting at the Bunch of Grapes or the Black Horse Tavern, they frequently collaborated on their output. "The American Anarchiad," published in 1786, ridiculed the anti-Federalists and the monarchists and extolled the virtues of a strong central government. Its concluding line was "Ye live united, or divided die." Alsop, Dwight and Dr. Hopkins composed an attack on the Jeffersonian Democrats for their sympathy with the French Revolution.

The liveliest work was John Trumbull's "M'Fingal," described as "a roaring, slapstick, rattling burlesque on the Tories." Its hero, the Loyalist Squire M'Fingal, is tarred, feathered and ridden out of town by an enraged mob. The satire caught the imagination of the reading public and went through 30 editions.

Joel Barlow devoted years to the writing of "The Columbiad" (1807), 5,000 lines of exuberant nationalism. In each edition he shocked his readers with forecasts of such improbable happenings as the construction of a canal across Panama and the elimination of the study of Greek and Latin in public schools.

TOP,
Joel Barlow.
Engraving.
ABOVE,
John Trumbull.
Engraving.
RIGHT,
"Tory's day of Judgement."
Engraving for M'Fingal, 1795.

Case, Lockwood & Brainard trade card, c. 1875.

Their adherence to the dying Federalist party doomed the Hartford Wits as a literary group, and their popularity was soon eclipsed by the appearance of individual American authors like James Fenimore Cooper and Washington Irving.

As early as 1820 Hartford had achieved national recognition as a publishing and printing center. Some 20 book and magazine publishers flourished. They employed 50,000 canvassers to travel about the country selling their books and magazines door-to-door. The first American children's magazine and first cookbook were Hartford creations. Subscription sales of up to 200,000 copies of popular titles were common. Hudson & Goodwin, owners of the *Courant,* made a large profit from editions of the *New England Primer* and Noah Webster's *Speller.* Newton Case founded a firm in 1836 that still exists under the name of Connecticut Printers. His success came from being the sole publisher for 15 years of Webster's *Dictionary,* the *Cottage Bible* and schoolbooks. By the 1880s, Case, Lockwood & Company was the largest printing house in the United States. Mark Twain had an interest in the American Publishing Company, which made money for him on three of his works, *Innocents Abroad, The Gilded Age* and *Tom Sawyer.* Before the end of the century the book business in Hartford faded away as New York became the center of publishing.

For a period of five years, from 1822 to 1827, Hartford had a poet of great promise in the person of John Brainard. A graduate of Yale, he came here to edit a newspaper called the *Mirror.* His most memorable poems dealt with the legends and beauties of the Connecticut Valley, especially the "Connecticut River." Unfortunately, he died of consumption in his 32nd year.

Long before Twain brought literary glamour to the city, several lesser lights made their mark as writers. Two of them were females. Emma Hart Willard, founder of the school for young ladies in Troy, New York that bears her name, resided in Hartford after her retirement and turned out textbooks on various subjects that sold a million copies. She also wrote poems, the best known of which is the "Ocean Hymn," containing the famous line, "Rocked in the cradle of the deep."

Lydia Huntley Sigourney was also an educator and poet who ran a seminary for young women in Hartford. Married to a banker who believed that wives should be seen but not read, she nevertheless poured out hundreds of saccharine verses for 50 years, with titles like "Death of an Infant," "Consecration of a Church," and "Baptism of an Infant at its Mother's Funeral." They were very popular with sentimental Victorians. The passing of any prominent Hartfordian was sure to inspire an effusive eulogy in verse. One of the oddest friendships in Hartford was between Lydia and Samuel Colt, probably because both were flamboyant characters and outstandingly successful money earners.

In the mid-19th century, Hartford had few literary luminaries. J. Hammond Trumbull was a noted historian, secretary of the state for Connecticut and president of The Connecticut Historical Society, who wrote extensively on Indian subjects and edited the first three volumes of the Connecticut Colony Records. Even more famous was the liberal preacher Horace Bushnell, whose religious works embodied a breadth of vision and beauty of style not unlike Emerson's writings. His masterpiece, published in 1859, was titled *Nature and the Supernatural.* Isaac W. Stuart, owner of the Wyllys Estate where stood the Charter Oak until 1856, won prominence as an orator, scholar and biographer of Nathan Hale and Jonathan Trumbull.

But for a renewal of the literary primacy that had died out with the Hartford Wits the city had to await the development of Nook Farm. In 1851 John Hooker of Farmington, a direct descendant of Thomas Hooker, purchased a tract of 100 acres at the western extremity of Farmington Avenue, the terminal point for the horse cars. He opened up Forest Street, built a substantial home and soon Nook Farm became the choicest residential district.

Here gathered a lively group of writers and activists—the prolific editor of the *Courant,* Charles Dudley Warner; America's first great woman novelist, Harriet Beecher Stowe; Senator Francis Gillette, whose son William created the stage version of Sherlock Holmes; the controversial suffragette Isabella Beecher Hooker; the preacher Joseph Twichell; General Joseph Hawley; and, of course, Mark Twain. In 1873 his distinctive Victorian house rose at the corner, described by a reporter as "the oddest piece of architecture . . . being a sort of cross between a Mexican adobe hut and a Swiss cottage, built of brick to cost about $40,000." The inhabitants of Nook Farm were a closely knit group, each member's home always being open to the others.

The Rev. Twichell was Twain's closest friend. Though the humorist never joined his congregation at the Asylum Hill Church, he did attend services regularly. Because so many of its members were bankers, insurance executives and stockbrokers, he dubbed it "the church of the holy speculators." The two men loved to take long walks and argue about religion and politics. On one occasion Twain confided that when he died, he wished to be cremated. "Oh," said Joe Twichell, "you won't have to worry about that, where you're going!"

Twain had a fascination for machinery, technology and capitalism that drove him to bankruptcy and despair, despite having earned more

Mark Twain House, Farmington Avenue, c. 1885.
BELOW,
Samuel L. Clemens (Mark Twain), c. 1885.

than $500,000 from his books, double the amount of any other American writer. Not only did he inherit an instinct for speculation, but he convinced himself he could become as successful a businessman as the insurance and manufacturing presidents he so greatly admired in the city which he called "the moneyed center of the state."

On his first visit to Hartford he toured Colt's Armory, where he was stunned by the "dense wilderness of strange iron machines" and enthusiastically tested Dr. Gatling's new machine gun. Some 20 years later he published *A Connecticut Yankee in King Arthur's Court,* both a savage satire and a paean to industry in which the hero is Colt's head superintendent. Undoubtedly modeled after Elisha K. Root, Colt's mechanical genius, the hero calls himself "a Yankee of the Yankees" who learned to make everything at the great arms factory.

Following the success of *Innocents Abroad,* the first of three books by Twain printed in Hartford by the American Publishing Company, the author bought stock in the firm and became a director. In 1880, when the publisher, Elisha Bliss, died, Twain withdrew his interest. But immediately he plunged, like a frantic gold seeker, into a series of speculations and inventions that drained his pocketbook and consumed his energies. He thought of himself as a captain of industry, as able as James G. Batterson or Morgan G. Bulkeley, and becoming a director of Hartford Fire must have bolstered his confidence. Making money was for him of paramount concern, because living on Nook farm in his splendid mansion was an expensive proposition and a constant worry. He sponsored dozens of inventions, some of them his own ideas, like the hinged pants button, pregummed scrapbook and razor strop. He gave a testimonial for the Remington typewriter, which he used, calling it "this curiosity-breeding little joker." Most of his days were cluttered with bothersome business details, and between 1884 and 1889 he published nothing at all.

Ironically, when embroiled in his most disastrous speculation, he turned down an opportunity that could have made him many times a millionaire. Alexander Graham Bell wanted him to invest in a new device called the telephone, but Twain considered the instrument an abomination. When his friends General Joseph Hawley and Charles Dudley Warner, the *Courant*'s editor, persuaded him to try it out, he reluctantly agreed, saying, "The voice carries too far as it is. If Bell had invented a muffler or a gag, he would have done a real service . . . He's crazy. Put the thing near the window so that I can get rid of it easily." His was the third phone installed in Hartford.

Twain threw away $25,000 to $30,000 each on such ideas as a patent steam generator, steam pulley and a new method of marine telegraphy. But these sums were chicken feed compared to his nemesis, the Paige typesetter. The complicated machine, containing 18,000 parts, promised to revolutionize the printing business. The author, captivated by its potential for making millions, invested $5,000 in 1880. Five years later, as the inventor contined to tinker, Twain began subsidizing its development at the rate of $3,000 a month. The years dragged on. Twain did his best to peddle stock, but his Hartford friends rebuffed him. Finally, in 1894 he had to accept the fact that the Paige typesetter was a lemon. Altogether, it cost him $180,000 of his book earnings. The shattering of his biggest dream soured him on business for the rest of his life. He wrote: "I think I am by nature and disposition unfit for it. My axiom is, to succeed in business, avoid my example."

Next door to Twain lived Mrs. Stowe, whose fame preceded her coming to live out her life on Forest Street. Her most famous book *Uncle Tom's Cabin* was undoubtedly the most influential anti-slavery novel published prior to the Civil War. Less well-known are her other tales about living in New England. She and her sister Catherine Beecher

Charles Dudley Warner.

Harriet Beecher Stowe.
Engraving, 1853.

*E.V. Mitchell's Bookstore.
Watercolor.*

wrote *The American Woman's Home* which contained many advanced ideas on home decor and household economy.

In 1891, when Twain closed the home he no longer could afford to maintain and moved his family to Europe, it marked the beginning of the dissolution of Nook Farm. Her mind failing, Mrs. Stowe wandered aimlessly in her neighbors' gardens, pulling off their best flowers, or slipping into their homes and playing sad melodies on their pianos. Five years later she died. The history of Nook Farm ended with the passing of the durable preacher Joseph Twichell in 1918.

Although it continued to produce gifted writers and artists, Hartford—and all of New England, for that matter—ceased to dominate the literary scene. The spinster daughter of J. Hammond Trumbull, Annie, was the best known and certainly the most energetic writer at the start of the 20th century. Her short stories were published in magazines like the *Atlantic Monthly* and *McClure's*, and she also wrote plays and novels. She belonged to many of the city's literary and social groups for women, of which the pinnacle was the Saturday Morning Club, founded in 1876 with the blessing and advice of Mark Twain.

Later appeared a small circle of regional writers like the poets Wilbert Snow and Robert Hillyer; the biographer Odell Shepard, professor of English at Trinity College; and Edwin Valentine Mitchell, who operated a bookstore and publishing house. In the back of his Lewis Street shop this coterie would gather on Saturday afternoons. One of the regulars for a while was Sinclair Lewis, who spent a year in Hartford in 1929, thinking about his next novel, *Arrowsmith*. Mitchell's partner was James Thrall Soby, the notable art critic and collector of modernist paintings who later became director of New York's Museum of Modern Art.

But the man who achieved the most fame posthumously was virtually an unknown in Hartford during his lifetime. Wallace Stevens, who won the Pulitzer Prize just before his death in 1955, led a double life, as a vice-president of the Hartford Accident & Indemnity Company and as the leading American poet of this century. On his first visit to Hartford in 1913 it was Annie Trumbull who entertained him and whom he described as "a most agreeable person, with very pleasant manners and a sense of humor."

Tall, good-looking and well-tailored, Stevens never mixed socially. William Carlos Williams, another poet, said "he was in the midst of a life crowded with business affairs a veritable monk . . . a frightened man drawing back from the world as if he had in fact been a New Englander." Stevens never explained his anti-social ways except to admit that "I want to keep everybody at arm's length in Hartford where I want nothing but the office and home as home." In all kinds of weather he used to walk the mile or so between his house on Westerly Terrace and his office. The purpose of this solitary commuting on foot was to compose, trying out poetic phrases like "the emperor of ice cream" or "the auroras of autumn."

A living Hartford-born writer of note is Brendan Gill, son of a physician and an editor of the *New Yorker* for a half century. Other local authors who have made their mark nationally are Oliver Butterworth, Jane Quigg and Elizabeth G. Spare, all writers of children's books, and Tom Tryon of Wethersfield, a novelist as well as an actor.

Eagle Tavern.

THE Subscriber feels grateful for the very liberal patronage he has received during his short residence in this City, and begs leave to inform his friends and the public generally, that he has raised his Eagle sign in front of the noted Tavern House recently occupied by Elisha Sears, which he intends fitting up as soon as the season will admit, in a superior style for the accommodation of travellers and others who may favor him with their custom.

Without going into a long detail of superior accommodations, the subscriber would merely state, that if good fare both for man and beast are any comfort to the weary traveller, he flatters himself it can no where be found in greater perfection than at the Eagle Tavern, where all favors will be thankfully received and gratefully acknowledged by the publick's much obliged and humble servant,

HARVEY MARSHALL.

Hartford, February, 1823.

GOODSELL & WELLS,—Printers.

In the 17th and 18th centuries the tavern or "ordinary" was the place to entertain and the center of community life. It functioned as a combination of bistro, saloon, Holiday Inn, courtroom, and exchange, a haven for weary travelers and a refuge for the local gentry. Here one could get warm, relax, imbibe, feast, gossip, inform and do business. And out back—in those plumbingless days—there had to be a "necessary," with at least two and sometimes four seats, to supplement the chamber pots in every room.

In 1784, when Hartford became a city, there were no less than 14 taverns, from the Black Horse to the Bunch of Grapes. Drunkenness was discouraged. There might be a sign in the taproom that read:

> Meet friendly,
> Drink moderately,
> Pay honestly,
> And part quietly.

When General Lafayette visited Hartford in 1780, he attended a dance in the ballroom of the Black Horse Tavern. President George Washington, on his tour of New England during the fall of 1789, lodged at David Bull's Bunch of Grapes on Main Street. There, three years later, a group of merchants met with Jeremiah Wadsworth to petition the Legislature for Connecticut's first bank charter. Amos Ransom's inn near the river had a handsome third-floor ballroom where fortnightly assemblies were held in wintertime for the city's elite. Moses Butler's tavern was a favorite meeting place for physicians and is given credit for being the cradle of the Hartford Medical Society.

The advent of the steamboat and the railroad gradually replaced the horse and stagecoach as the primary means of travel and in turn led to the decline of taverns. In Hartford hotels and restaurants took their place, while saloons catered to the immigrants. In 1845, under the

ABOVE,
Tavern sign for John Spencer,
1810.
Painted wood.
FAR LEFT,
Eagle Tavern broadside, 1823.
BELOW,
Billhead, Ripley's United States
Hotel, State Street.
Engraving, c. 1828.

United States Hotel, Honiss' restaurant opened, and in 1860 appeared the Marble Pillar. Both are still in existence. Honiss specialized in seafood, while the Marble Pillar featured bratwurst, sauerbraten and other German delicacies; whisky was five cents, with eels and kippers served free. During the Civil War the latter served as a recruiting center. About 1890 the Heublein Hotel, where A-1 sauce originated, became a favorite dining spot.

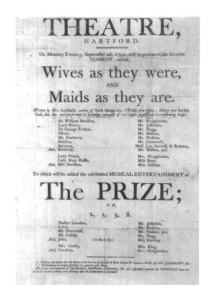

RIGHT,
*Heublein Hotel.
Postcard, c. 1910.*
BELOW,
*Hartford Theatre broadside,
1799.*

Popular entertainment began in the taverns and coffee houses. The first recorded indoor entertainment was a waxworks display in 1788 at the Bunch of Grapes. There followed such exotic spectacles as camels imported from Arabia, clever monkeys, trained dogs and musical clocks. In 1795 the first real circus, "with riders, dancers and a clown" appeared. The city's first resident portrait painter, Joseph Steward, set up a museum of curiosities in the State House.

Theatrical entertainment, on the other hand, was regarded by most Hartfordians as improper if not immoral well into the Gilded Age. The earliest effort was an amateur show staged at the first State House in May 1788 by a daring group of Yale juniors before an audience of gentlemen and clergymen "who were very much offended by the profane language introduced." The same year a dramatic performance took place at Bull's Tavern, and in the following decade traveling companies presented several plays. From 1795 through 1799 the city had a theater of its own, erected by Ephraim Root on Temple Street with the financial help of 57 very proper citizens including the Wadsworths, John Morgan, Barzillai Hudson and Peleg Sanford. Aware of the prejudices of their patrons, the actors from New York assured them that their entertainments would be "a source of moral instruction as well as of amusement. . . ." The theater was a plain hall with chandeliers that dripped hot wax on the customers, with footlights lit by candles and a green baize curtain. The latter came down permanently when in 1800 the General Assembly passed "An Act to Prevent Theatrical Shows and Entertainments" throughout the state.

The dramatic drought lasted half a century until the Legislature reversed itself and allowed local option. George H. Wyatt's Lyceum was

the first to take advantage of the new law in 1853, using the American Hall, but it soon failed. The vacuum was filled by Touro Hall, a former church acquired by the Jews that accommodated 1,500 people and was rented for public meetings, entertainments and stores. Roberts Opera House opened on Main Street in 1869 and was soon joined by the Allyn Theater on Trumbull Street, where the Civic Center now stands. On Nook Farm Mark Twain encouraged the son of his neighbor, Senator Francis Gillette, in his theatrical ambitions. William Gillette's first part was in a dramatization of Twain's *The Gilded Age*. When the play came to the Allyn Theater in 1875, with Will in the cast, the residents of Nook Farm turned out in force to cheer his performance. Their support was a major factor in making theater respectable. Another major event in Hartford's theatrical life was the opening of Parsons Theater on Central Row in 1896, which attracted the best shows and actors for many years.

Like theater, music took a much longer time to develop because of puritanical attitudes. As late as 1815 an ordinance was passed prohibiting the beating of drums or playing of horns after sunset. Early in the 1800s, however, there were organs in a few churches and one in the State House Museum that competed with its waxworks, paintings and artifacts. The first organ, locally built, was installed in Christ Church. Concerts of sacred music and songs were well attended. In 1807 nearly 100 singers performed Handel's "Messiah" at the dedication of the new Center Church sanctuary, said to be the first rendition of the Hallelujah Chorus in America.

Until after 1816 public concerts were rare. These featured Scotch and Irish ballads at places like Morgan's coffee house and Ripley's United States Hotel, frequently sung by traveling artists from abroad. The first Choral Society appeared in 1822. In the 1840s family groups like the popular Hutchinson quartet often sang in the city, and in 1846 the first operatic prima donna, Signora Rosina Pico, inaugurated the opening of American Hall. The coming of Jenny Lind, the Swedish nightingale, in 1851 caused a minor riot. The Fourth Church (Horace Bushnell's) was twice oversold, and people sought seats on nearby window ledges and roofs. So enthusiastic were some and so frustrated the rest that Miss Lind had to jump out of a rear window to escape the overwrought crowd. Later on saw the formation of musical societies and orchestras, like the Musical Club of 1892, which is still alive.

Hartford residents began to play in earnest during the prosperous

TOP,
Parsons Theater.
ABOVE,
William Gillette and Arthur Byron in a scene from "Samson" at Parsons Theater, 1909.
RIGHT,
Balloon launching in Hartford, July 4, 1863.

years following the Civil War, a period Mark Twain and Charles Dudley Warner scathingly called the "Gilded Age," when many of the old Puritan inhibitions and prejudices were shed. Reduction of the workday from 12 to 10 hours left some leisure time for even the poorest. Sports and entertainment of all kinds became acceptable activities.

Excursion steamers, like the *Frolic* and *Sunshine*, carried passengers up and down the river and even across Long Island Sound. Swimming and sailing were also popular before the water became too polluted from the wastes discharged by the towns and industries along the Connecticut's banks. In 1895, the Hartford Yacht Club, third oldest in the country, hosted participants in weekend sailing races.

Charter Oak Park, now the site of Colt Industries in West Hartford, used to draw thousands to its fairs, carnivals, trotting and automobile races until the Great Depression. Back in 1876 Hartford made sports history when its leading citizen, Morgan G. Bulkeley, became a founder and first president of the National Baseball League.

During the Gay '90s the bicycling craze began in Hartford with the

TOP,
Steamer "Sunshine" on the Connecticut River.
ABOVE,
Racedriver Eddie Ball at Charter Oak Park, 1906.
RIGHT,
Charter Oak Park program. Lithograph, 1888.

founding of the Pope Manufacturing Company, in its heyday the city's largest industry and the originator of the "safety" two-wheeler. Bicycle clubs sprang up, and energetic young men engaged in "century runs," a 100-mile jaunt through the countryside. Bicycle lawn parties were fashionable.

Basketball made its debut at the Y.M.C.A., where office clerks and factory workers could spend their nonworking hours playing cards—not for money—in wholesome Christian surroundings. When it came to Christian living, however, the ladies were ahead of the men: they built the first Y.W.C.A. dormitory in the country on Church Street in 1867.

By the Roaring '20s Hartford had almost everything in sports: horse racing, baseball, tennis, golf, track, polo, football, and—perhaps most exciting of all—boxing. Three sons of Hartford families became world champions: "Bat" Battalino, Willie Pep and "Kid" Kaplan.

Cultural pursuits also began in earnest after the Civil War with the formation of literary clubs for men and women. Mark Twain and other intellectuals were members of the exclusive Monday Evening Club, and Twain acted as mentor for the Saturday Morning Club "to promote Culture and Social Intercourse" among young misses. Men clubbed together to satisfy special interests. The Irish launched the Hartford

ABOVE,
W. H. (Billy) Rhodes of the Hartford Wheel Club, 1886.
ABOVE RIGHT,
Ladies Cycle Club, 1890.
RIGHT,
Working men's Exchange at the Y.M.C.A.

Louis "Kid" Kaplan, World's Featherweight Champion 1925–27, 1948.

branch of the Ancient Order of Hibernians in 1871, which at one time boasted of having 1,000 members. In 1879 five enthusiastic canoeists established the Hartford Canoe Club for "the physical and intellectual improvement of its members," a purpose never seriously regarded as it became a privileged male haven for drinking, dining and more drinking. The journal of the Saturday Morning Club pointed out, in 1891, that "club life is the order of the day . . . We are yielding to the Spirit of the Age, which demands combination and the fusion of ideas."

Since its founding in 1873, members of the Hartford Club have represented the business elite of the city, and until the turn of the century it served as the center of social life outside the home. It is still a focal point for board meetings, company parties, testimonial dinners, business conferences, celebrity speakers and other events. Within its private dining rooms have been held countless meetings affecting corporate and philanthropic decision-making. Hartford's two other eating clubs are the University Club (1906) and the Town and County Club, owned and operated by women for women, which opened in 1925.

By the time of World War I, movies provided a new form of family entertainment. Of the city's several downtown movie houses the most splendid was Loew's-Poli on Main Street, now the site of Bushnell Towers. Next door to the theater stood Besse's ice cream parlor. Those who desired the best dessert for a party or Sunday dinner ordered Besse's ice cream delicacies to be delivered to their homes in salt-packed containers. One by one the movie palaces began to disappear in the 1960s. The Strand was the last to go in 1974.

The performing arts in Hartford took a giant step forward in the 1930s when three important events occurred. First was the opening of the Bushnell Memorial Hall on January 13, 1930. Two nights later a half-century tradition of symphony concerts by visiting orchestras began with a performance by the Philadelphia Orchestra under the direction of Leopold Stokowski. The Bushnell's first managing director was William H. Mortensen, who ran the Hall with great charm and skill for 38 years.

Four years later came the modernistic Avery Memorial wing of the Wadsworth Atheneum. For its opening the *avant garde* director, A. Everett Austin Jr., staged the world premiere of an opera by Gertrude Stein and Virgil Thompson, called "Four Saints in Three Acts," with sets by Salvadore Dali. In November of that year the first public concert of the newly-organized Hartford Symphony was held in the Avery Memorial Auditorium. More than any other individual, Francis Goodwin II was the father of the symphony, which moved to the Bushnell in 1936 and has played there ever since.

Years later another Goodwin, James L., who lived in the family's Gothic "castle" that once stood on the corner of Asylum Avenue and Woodland Street, was the chief benefactor of the Austin Arts Center at Trinity College. Hartford's two other leading performing arts organizations are the Connecticut Opera Association, founded in 1950 by Frank Pandolfi, a music teacher turned impresario, and the Hartford Ballet, first directed by Joseph Albano in 1960. In 1971 the Greater Hartford Arts Council was created to raise money annually for all artistic endeavors.

After the demise of both the old Parsons Theater in 1936 and the New Parsons in 1953, Hartford lacked an outlet for legitimate stage plays until the formation of the Hartford Stage Company in 1964. Its first two directors were Jacques Cartier and Paul R. Weidner. In 1977

the Stage Company moved to a new 489-seat home on Church Street. Other theater groups which operate successfully in the city are the Mark Twain Masquers, the Producing Guild and the Lincoln Theater on the campus of the University of Hartford.

Numerous Hartford-born have achieved fame on stage, screen and television. William Gillette, son of Senator Francis Gillette, became famous for his role as Sherlock Holmes; Sophie Tucker was loved as a songstress and "red-hot mama"; Ed Begley won an Oscar for his performance in the movie "Sweet Bird of Youth"; Katharine Hepburn—winner of four Oscars—is still making films after 55 years of acting; Norman Lear, creator of "All In The Family," is a leading TV producer. Other show business personalities from Hartford include Mike Yellin, Marietta Canty, Ann Corio, Gary Merrill, Louis Nye, Rita Gahn Morley, Peter Falk, Totie Fields, Charles N. Reilly and Katharine Houghton.

In the 1970s the Greater Hartford Chamber of Commerce and the City Council agreed that the city needed a multipurpose civic center. Aetna Life & Casualty put up $35 million for a shopping mall, and the city floated a $30.5 million bond issue to build the 15,000 seat auditorium and exhibition hall. The Civic Center was completed in 1975 and is the home of the National Hockey League's Hartford Whalers.

Of major concern to Hartford residents is the "quality of life." Not only has the city, on the whole, been a good place in which to make a living, but in recent years it has aspired to excel in the enjoyment of living. Basic to this goal is an environment of clean air, pure water and open space, together with multiple opportunities to participate in cultural and leisure-time activities.

From a physical standpoint Hartford has been unusually fortunate, considering its relatively small geographic area, in having so much room for outdoor play—over 2,100 acres devoted to parks, greens and playgrounds. In addition, its eastern boundary consists of 6.6 miles of riverfront, a long-neglected resource for recreation that happily is now being recognized. In 1980 Riverfront Recapture, Inc. was formed and a master plan developed to bring people back to the Connecticut River by means of riverwalks on both sides, a pedestrian walkway across the river, a permanent dock, and eventually a downtown plaza over the interstate highway.

*This engraving by J.G. Kellogg of
a raging fire in the Mitchell
Building on State Street was used
on the membership certificate of
the Fireman's Benevolent Society
organized in 1836.*

TOP,
*Aftermath of explosion at Fales &
Gray Car Works, March 2, 1854.*
BELOW,
*Broadside, meeting to organize
aid for victims of the Fales &
Gray disaster, March 3, 1854.*
MIDDLE RIGHT,
*Flood of May 1, 1854, State
Street.*
Lithograph, 1854.
BELOW and RIGHT,
*Views of the Colt Armory fire,
1864.*

It has long been said of this Insurance City that here all disasters are "doubly mourned"! For good reason Hartford's insurance companies have emphasized safety and accident prevention as well as the selling of insurance policies.

Fire fighting and fire insurance are two of Hartford's oldest professions. From 1789, when the fire department was formed, until the Civil War, firemen were volunteers. The law required every householder to keep on hand a leather fire bucket. At the sound of the alarm, he toted it to the fire. There, filled with water, it could be passed from hand to hand along a double line of similarly equipped citizens.

In 1854 the explosion of a brand new Woodruff & Beach steam boiler in the Fales & Gray Car Works resulted in 21 deaths and more than 50 injured persons. The accident led to the founding of both the Hartford Hospital and the Hartford Steam Boiler Inspection and Insurance Company.

Flooding on the Connecticut River, especially in springtime, has always been a major problem for the city. In the great flood of 1854, which crested at nearly 29 feet, the South Meadows and Colt's Armory were saved by a two-mile long dike completed just in time by Colonel Colt. The rest of the city was badly inundated as can be seen here.

In February of 1864 one of the worst calamities ever to befall a Hartford industry occurred. The original Colt Armory with its unique blue onion dome burned to the ground. Nine hundred men were thrown out of work just as Colt revolvers and muskets were most needed by General Grant's armies. The disaster, however, did goad the city fathers to establish a paid fire department.

First revered by the Indians because of its great size, the Charter Oak has symbolized freedom ever since that dark October evening in 1687 when it served its historic purpose of sheltering Connecticut's Royal Charter. By the middle of the 19th century the gnarled base of the tree measured over 33 feet in circumference. During a violent windstorm on the night of August 21, 1856, the old tree fell. Colt's Band played funeral dirges at the site, and poetess Lydia Sigourney penned a long eulogy.

An architectural disaster occurred in 1882 when a new U.S. Post Office was built on the east lawn of the Old State House. Fortunately, it was torn down in 1933 and a new Post Office erected on High Street (now the William R. Cotter Federal Building).

Few oldsters are still alive to recall the Blizzard of '88, which paralyzed the city for days.

Main Street, Blizzard of 1888.

A generation after the Fales & Gray explosion, another disaster occurred from the same cause. The Park Central, a rather decrepit, five-story hotel on Allyn Street, catered to permanent boarders and traveling salesmen. The owner, Wellington Ketchem, his wife and black-and-tan dog also lived there.

In room 10 on the second floor Lizzie Guilder, a regular boarder, woke up at 4:30 on Sunday morning, February 17, 1889. She was thirsty. Opening her door, she saw George Gaines, the black porter, passing along the hall and asked him to bring her a pitcher of ice water. After what seemed a long wait, she stepped into the hall and through the speaking tube called down to Edward Perry, the night clerk. Just as she turned away from the tube, Lizzie felt the floor rise under her feet and a rush of air pushed her toward the door of her room. At the same moment she heard a sharp explosion followed by an earthquake-like shock. Seizing her hat and coat, she ran back into the hall as it collapsed under her feet and escaped by a stairway in the annex. Downstairs behind his counter Perry was instantly killed, while the porter met the same fate in the act of getting Miss Guilder's water.

Soon after Miss Guilder's escape the mail clerk from the depot was running at full speed past the hotel toward the engine house to give the alarm, when he was accosted by a man wearing a plug hat, a balbriggan wrapper and his underclothes. "Tell me, young fellow, where can I find the home of a clerk who works in a clothing store?" By this time the hotel had sunk into a mass of burning rubbish. Except for the eastern wing not one brick remained intact. The engineer on duty, William Seymour, had forgotten to maintain the water level in the boiler. He too was a casualty.

Daylight revealed a terrifying scene, firemen playing their hoses, bodies protruding from the debris, rescuers already probing the remains. It was a dreary morning, rainy and chilly. As in every catastrophe the curious began to gather early. Before the end of the day extra cars had to be attached to trains from Windsor and New Britain to carry those who yearned to see death and destruction at first hand. Governor Bulkeley called out four companies of the National Guard, alerting them by twice 11 strokes of the fire bell, to drive back the sightseers.

Aftermath of Park Central Hotel explosion, February, 1889.

Soon there were 300 hundred men working with ropes, crowbars and bare hands.

Shortly after noon Walter Gray, a traveler for the Higganum Manufacturing Company, was rescued still lying in bed. According to his account, he didn't hear the explosion but awoke among falling bricks. Though pinned down by a heavy beam and a jumble of lathe and plaster, he was unhurt and able to breathe through the thick smoke. What really worried him was that he might drown from the water being poured onto the fire; it rose up to his shoulders. Shivering from head to toe, he declared himself ready to go to work if only he could get some clothes.

After being buried for eight hours the proprietor, his wife and dog were also brought out safely. Another couple, Mr. and Mrs. Maximilian Galody, were not so lucky; the publisher of the Hartford *Herald,* Galody was a German immigrant who had been in the city only a few years. Warmed by 280 gallons of coffee, the rescuers labored until 2 o'clock the next morning. They found 10 persons still alive, but 22 bodies, some charred beyond recognition, were uncovered and carried to the nearby office of Dr. O.C. Smith for identification.

In the 1890s the Pride of Hartford, then the largest self-propelled steam fire engine in the world, frightened the horses on Main Street.

The wooden covered bridge to East Hartford was unique in having a trolley track. Originally built in 1809, it was the second bridge across the Connecticut River, the first being at Enfield. Rebuilt in 1818, it was destroyed by fire in 1895 and replaced by the present Bulkeley Bridge in 1908. For a while ferry service had to be revived.

On Saturday, July 8, 1905, this runaway locomotive smashed through the wall of the New York, New Haven & Hartford Railroad's roundhouse, then located on the site of the present State Armory.

In 1897 Travelers Insurance Company wrote the first automobile insurance policy, and for good reason! Here is an unusual documentation of the New Haven site of the first fatal car accident in the state.

February 21, 1914, a bitter, wintry day, Union Station caught fire.

Tommy Guilfoil, a proud Hartford fireman.

One of the city's largest conflagrations burned out G. Fox & Co. in 1917. All records were destroyed, making it necessary for customers to pay their bills from memory.

No one then living will ever forget the flood of March 1936, the biggest flood of all. The river reached a height of 37.6 feet, destroyed $35,000,000 worth of property and took 11 lives. Large sections of the city were inundated, making Colt's Armory an island.

July 6, 1944, was a day of great tragedy in Hartford. The main tent of Ringling Brothers Circus caught fire. In just a few minutes, 168 men, women and children perished. Many more suffered burns and other injuries. The body of one little girl about six years of age was never claimed. Perhaps her parents, too, died in the fire. She was buried in a cemetery near Hartford. Every July 6, Memorial Day and Christmas, Detective Lieutenant Thomas C. Barber and retired Detective Sargeant Edward T. Lowe brought flowers to decorate the grave of "Little Miss 1565" during their lifetime.

On December 31, 1956 fire gutted the old Cathedral of St. Joseph.

Early in the morning of January 7, 1978 the "space frame" roof over the coliseum in the Civic Center collapsed, only hours after thousands had attended a basketball game. Fortunately, there were no injuries. It was replaced by a conventional truss-type roof.

The City's Worst Fires and Catastrophes

Year	Location	Loss
1766	Powder explosion	6 killed
1853	Trinity Roman Catholic Church	total
1854	Fales & Gray car works explosion	21 killed, 50 injured
	Downtown flooded; river crested at 29 feet, 10 inches	
1858	Willis Thrall screw factory	$ 112,000
1864	Colt's Armory	$ 200,000; 1 death
1867	Hartford & N.Y. Steamboat Co. warehouse	$ 100,000
1872	Colt's willow-ware works	$ 68,000
1875	St. Patrick Church	$ 100,000
1877	Ford Street building	$ 225,000
1878	Kohn block	3 firemen killed
1882	Hartford Public High School	$ 190,000
1887	George O. Sawyer's store	$ 121,700; 1 dead
1888	Great Blizzard	
1889	Park Central Hotel	22 killed
1892	Ætna Pyrotechnic Works	5 killed
1894	Colt's Armsmear	$ 73,000
1895	Covered bridge to East Hartford burned	
1902	Capewell Horse Nail Co.	$ 500,000
1907	Central N. E. Railway Co.	$ 80,000
1914	Union Station	$ 160,000
1917	G. Fox & Co.	$ 700,000
	Loydon, Northam & Loydon building	$ 100,000
1920	Jewell Court	$ 200,000

1921	Crown Theater & Main St. garage	$ 150,000
1923	Collapse of Fuller Brush tower	10 killed
1926	Hartford Club	$ 75,000
	East Hartford railroad yards	$ 275,000
	East Hartford tobacco growers	$ 700,000
	Hartford Retreat	1 killed
1927	Clarkin baseball field	$ 80,000
	Connecticut River rose to 29 feet, third highest record	
1930	Miller building	$ 90,000; 1 killed
1932	Herrup's furniture store	$ 250,000
1936	Great flood; record height of 37 feet, 6 inches	
1938	First hurricane in 123 years	$7.4 million damages; 4,000 homeless
1939	Steamboat dock	$ 50,000
1941	Ropkin's brewery	$ 100,000
	Collapse of Charter Oak bridge	15 dead
1944	Ringling Brothers Circus Fire	168 dead
1945	Niles Street Hospital	21 dead
1949	Arsenal School	$ 75,000
1949	Cleveland block	$ 150,000
1955	South Congregational Church	$ 50,000
	Two floods	
1956	St. Patrick's Church	$ 250,000
	St. Joseph Cathedral	$5,000,000
1959	Cleveland building	$ 165,000
1961	Hartford Hospital	$ 300,000; 16 dead
1978	Collapse of Civic Center Roof	

Stone Bridge, over Park River.
Lithograph, c. 1834.

Significant Events

1633	"House of Good Hope" trading post established by Dutch.
1635–1636	Arrival of Puritan settlers from Massachusetts Bay to Connecticut to found Hartford.
1637	Pequot War fought. Defeat of the Indians brought peace to the Connecticut Colony.
1638/1639	Hooker delivered the sermon which asserted that the foundation of authority lay in "the free consent of the people," as a result of which Hartford adopted the "Fundamental Orders," the first written constitution in the world and the beginning of American democracy.
1647	Hartford hanged New England's first witch.
1654	Dutch driven out of Hartford.
1662	John Winthrop Jr. obtained a royal charter for Connecticut.
1687	Governor Edmund Andros of New England assumed rule over Connecticut, but the Charter was hidden until his removal two years later.
1745	About 100 Hartford men took part in the capture of Louisbourg, the French fortress on Cape Breton Island.
1764	The first issue of the weekly *Connecticut Courant* was published, making the *Courant* the oldest newspaper in continuous publication in America.
1771	Formation of the Governor's Foot Guard, the oldest military organization in the United States in continuous existence.
1782	Emergence of the Hartford Wits, the nation's first literary group.
1783	America's first copyright law enacted at Hartford. Publication of Webster's blue-backed Speller by Hudson & Goodwin. Jupiter Hammon, a Hartford native, became the first published black poet in America.
1784	City of Hartford incorporated.
1788	Hartford Woolen Manufactory, first woolen mill in America.
1790	First Baptist church organized.
1792	Founding of Hartford Bank, now Connecticut National Bank. Christ Church erected, which served Episcopalians until 1829.
1794	Smith Worthington, oldest manufacturer of saddles and harnesses, formed.
1796	Completion of the Old State House designed by Charles Bulfinch.
1797	Dr. Apollos Kinsley of Hartford built the first steam road wagon ever operated.
1798	America's first Home Missionary Society organized.
1800	John Graham demonstrated in Barnard Park his passenger-carrying air balloons, which the *Courant* called "vertical air coaches."
1807	Center Church's (1636) fourth meeting house erected on Main Street; Daniel Wadsworth reputed to be the architect. Noah Webster published earliest version of his American dictionary.

1809	Opening of toll bridge to East Hartford.
	Organization of Hartford Female Beneficent Society, first institution for care of orphans.
1810	Hartford Fire, first organized insurance company, chartered by Daniel Wadsworth, Daniel Buck and David Watkinson.
	Daniel Wadsworth built first lookout tower for public use on Talcott Mountain.
1811	Birth of the great educator Henry Barnard, who became the first U.S. Commissioner of Education in 1867.
1812	War with England.
1814	Founding of Phoenix State Bank, predecessor of Connecticut Bank and Trust Company, Hartford's second oldest.
	Hartford Convention held in Old State House.
1815	First steamboat voyage up the Connecticut River to Hartford.
1817	Thomas Gallaudet founded the American School for the Deaf, first institution for the handicapped in the Western Hemisphere.
	Hartford Times founded; it ceased publication in 1976.
1818	State constitution drafted at the Old State House, disestablishing the Congregational Church.
1819	Society for Savings organized; also Aetna Insurance Company.
1820	First Methodist Episcopal Church.
	With 20 publishing houses, Hartford became the center of book publishing in the United States.
1822	Hartford Retreat, now the Institute for Living, organized, oldest hospital in Connecticut and third oldest in the country.
1823	Washington College, renamed Trinity College in 1845, founded as the first institution of higher learning to state in its charter that no student should be excluded because of religious affiliation.
1824	General Lafayette paid a farewell visit to the city.
1825	Founding of The Connecticut Historical Society as part of Wadsworth Atheneum.
1826	Pliny Jewell made first leather belting for transmitting power to machines.
1827	Organization of first black church (now Faith Congregational) on Talcott Street.
	Organized in 1670, the South Congregational Church built its present brick edifice on lower Main Street.
1829	Roman Catholics bought their first church in Hartford from the Episcopalians for the sum of $900, calling it Church of the Holy Trinity.
	Construction of Christ Church Cathedral on Main Street.
	Henry Hudson installed a Fourdrinier machine for making fine grain paper.
1831	Alexis de Tocqueville visited Hartford, inspecting the American School for the Deaf and the new state prison in Wethersfield.
	Covenant Mutual Insurance Company founded.
1832	Levi Lincoln of Phoenix Iron Works invented a machine for making and inserting wire teeth in cards used to produce cotton and woolen goods, thus eliminating hand labor.
1833	A.M.E. church organized.
1834	New stone bridge on Main Street was the largest yet built in the United States.

1836	Reputation of Hartford insurance companies for integrity and reliability recognized when Hartford Fire paid in full all claims resulting from a devastating fire in New York that destroyed 700 buildings.
	First American patent for friction matches awarded to Alonzo D. Phillips of Hartford, whose factory was located on Front Street.
1838	Young Men's Institute, later Hartford Public Library, founded.
	Railroad completed between New Haven and Hartford.
1839	Highway to New Haven opened.
	Hartford Public High School, second oldest (1638) in the United States, erected its original schoolhouse on Asylum Avenue. HPHS moved to Forest Street in 1963.
1842	Wadsworth Atheneum, the country's first public art museum, established.
	Charles Dickens, visiting Hartford, complained that "too much of the old Puritan spirit" still existed.
1843	Founding of Beth Israel, first synagogue in Hartford and Connecticut.
1844	Dr. Horace Wells, Hartford dentist, first to use nitrous oxide as an anesthetic.
	First Unitarian Congregational Society of Hartford organized.
1846	Connecticut Mutual Life Insurance Company founded, first of its kind.
	The Rogers brothers invented first electroplating machine for silverware.
1847	G. Fox & Company opened its doors, Hartford's first department store.
1848	Christian Sharps received a patent for first successful breech-loading rifle.
	Founding of Hartford City Gas Light Company, now Connecticut Natural Gas.
1849	Railroad station built at street level; tracks raised in 1887.
1851	Founding of Phoenix Mutual Life Insurance Company, which initially insured only teetotallers.
	Jenny Lind, the "Swedish Nightingale," the first great European singer to come to America, sang in Hartford.
	Formation of the Ararat Lodge of B'nai B'rith, the Jewish social and benevolent brotherhood.
1852	Y.M.C.A. opened.
1853	Aetna Life Insurance Company started.
1854	City built reservoir on Lord's Hill and pumped water from the Connecticut River.
	Bushnell Park created, first municipally owned park in the world.
	Major flood inundated city, cresting at 29.8 feet, the worst on record until 1936.
	Hartford Hospital chartered as result of Fales & Gray boiler explosion.
	West Hartford separated from city of Hartford.
1855	Samuel Colt began operations in the Colt Armory, the largest private gun-making establishment in the world.
	Pitkin Brothers Iron Works invented first galvanized pipe for city water lines, eliminating the danger of lead poisoning.

1856   Fall of Charter Oak tree (in which was hidden the Connecticut Colony's Charter of 1662 from 1687–1689).

1858   Incorporation of Watkinson Library, now housed at Trinity College.
Opening of State Bank for Savings.

1859   Hartford-Wethersfield Horse Railroad Company chartered; in 1895 it became a trolley line.

1860   Pratt & Whitney Machine Tool Company founded.
Founding of Boys' Club of Hartford.
Abraham Lincoln made a campaign speech to his supporters, whom he dubbed the "Wide Awakes."

1861   Chartering of Mechanics Savings Bank.

1862   Charles Billings and Christoper Spencer invented first efficient drop forging machine.

1863   Travelers Insurance Companies founded. First American accident insurance issued to James Bolter of Hartford. The next year, first casualty policy issued to Hartford coal dealer Edwin S. Tyler in amount of $5,000 to cover his trip to Washington, D.C. The premium was $2.00.

1864   Colt Armory burned to the ground, as a result of which the city established a paid fire department.

1865   Connecticut General Life Insurance Company founded.

1866   The Hartford Steam Boiler Inspection and Insurance Company chartered, first to insure boilers.
Asylum Hill Congregational Church dedicated.

1867   Y.W.C.A. founded, first in the country to have a dormitory.

1869   Cornerstone for First Presbyterian Church (organized 1851) laid.
Opening of Roberts Opera House on Main Street.

1871   Valley Railroad opened from Hartford to Saybrook.
Union Baptist Church began worship in a discarded boxcar on Spruce Street.

1872   German Catholics organized and later built Sacred Heart Church.
Union for Home Work founded, oldest ancestor of Hartford Neighborhood Centers.
Trinity College's new Gothic-style campus laid out.
Cheney Brothers' mall erected on Main Street, now the Richardson Building.

1874   Mark Twain occupied his new home on Farmington Avenue.
Hartford Club incorporated.

1875   Hartford made sole capital of Connecticut.
Cornerstone laid for first Jewish synagogue in Connecticut, Temple Beth Israel, on Charter Oak Avenue.

1876   Morgan G. Bulkeley, founded the National Baseball League.
Christopher Spencer invented first automatic turret lathe, leading to formation of Hartford Machine Screw Company.

1878   First Columbia bicycle produced by Weed Sewing Machine Company on Capitol Avenue for Colonel Pope.
First dirigible flight in United States took place in Hartford.

1879   New capitol building finished.

| 1879 | For Pratt & Whitney, W.A. Rogers and George M. Bond invented the Rogers-Bond Comparator, a measuring device accurate to 1/50,000 of an inch. |

1879   For Pratt & Whitney, W.A. Rogers and George M. Bond invented the Rogers-Bond Comparator, a measuring device accurate to 1/50,000 of an inch.
Smyth Manufacturing Company organized to produce bookbinding machinery, invented by David M. Smyth.

1881   Hartford Electric Light Company chartered.
George Capewell invented first automatic machine for making horsenails.

1883   First photographs (of Civil War generals) for advertising used by Travelers Insurance.

1884   Watkinson Juvenile & Farm School opened on Park Street.
Moses C. Johnson invented first friction clutch.
Open Hearth Mission founded on Sheldon Street.

1886   Dedication of Soldiers & Sailors Memorial Arch on Trinity Street.
William Gray invented first coin-operated telephone.
Board of Trade, predecessor to the Chamber of Commerce, formed.
Founding of Hartford Art School.

1888   Great Blizzard on March 12 paralyzed city; 30 inches of snow fell in four days.

1889   Boiler explosion in Park Central Hotel killed 22.

1892   Consecration of St. Joseph Cathedral.

1893   Hartford Electric Light first utility to transmit three-phase alternating current and in 1896 first to install underground cable.

1894   Curtis Veeder invented first American cyclometer.

1895   Completion of Hartford's park system by Francis Goodwin.
Wooden bridge across the river burned. Manufacture of first pneumatic tire.

1896   Elizabeth Park, the country's oldest municipal rose garden, laid out. It was opened in 1903.
Opening of Parsons Theater.

1897   Travelers Insurance issued first automobile policy to Gilbert J. Loomis of Westfield.
Pope Manufacturing Company began manufacture of automobiles.
Founding of St. Francis Hospital.

1898   Opening of St. Thomas Seminary.
Italian community organized St. Anthony's parish.
Erection of Keney Memorial Clock Tower, first monument in this country to honor a mother.

1899   John T. Austin founded Austin Organ Company to produce his Universal Air Chest Organ. He also invented a machine for perforating paper used on player pianos and organs.

1901   Nation's first speed limit law enacted (12 m.p.h., 8 m.p.h. in city).
Underwood Typewriter moved to Hartford.

1903   Erection of Sts. Cyril & Methodius Church by Polish community on Charter Oak Avenue; also Lithuanians consecrated their Holy Trinity Church.

1904   Connecticut's first Christian Science Church built.

1905   Hartford Electric Light installed world's first central station steam turbine.

Children posing on Charles Street, 1906.

1906   Investing $400, Alfred C. Fuller evolved idea of a twisted-in-wire brush, leading to the Fuller Brush Company.
        Incorporation of University Club on Lewis Street.

1907   New Bulkeley Bridge opened to the public. Its dedication the next year drew 250,000 persons.
        City Plan Commission formed.
        Home office of Travelers Insurance constructed.

1908   Royal Typewriter opened its plant.

1909   Trolley lines extended to Bloomfield and Middletown.
        State Armory, capable of seating 10,000, completed.
        Hiram P. Maxim invented first successful gun silencer.

1910   Morgan Memorial wing of Wadsworth Atheneum erected.
        Completion of new State Library and Supreme Court building.

1911   Asylum Street, from Main to Trumbull, became a "Great White Way" with its new street lights.

1912   Jewish Family Service formed by 30 charitable groups.

1913   J.M. Ney introduced gold alloys to the dental profession.
        Isle of Safety built on State Street.

1914   Dedication of new Municipal Building.
        Union Station destroyed by fire.

1915   Founding of American Radio Relay League by Hiram P. Maxim.

1916   Kingswood School for Boys started, Hartford's first private country-day school, now Kingswood-Oxford for boys and girls.

1917   Inventor John Browning perfected for Colt's his Browning machine gun, automatic rifle and automatic pistol.
        G. Fox & Company burned, suffering a loss of $750,000.
        Coldest winter ever recorded.

1918   Karl Peiler patented the first automatic bottle-making machine for Emhart.
        First airmail received in Hartford.

1919   Travelers Insurance offered first aircraft liability coverage. The company's tower was completed, until 1984 the tallest building between Boston and New York.

1920   Hartford Electric started construction of South Meadows power plant.
        Connecticut becomes last state to ratify Woman's Suffrage amendment.

1921   Junior League of Hartford founded.
        Dedication of Brainard Airport, second oldest municipal airfield in United States.

1923   Collapse of Fuller Brush Tower killed 10 persons.
        League of Women Voters established.
        Hartford Electric Light operated first mercury turbine.
        Opening of Mt. Sinai Hospital.

1924   Hartford's first radio station, WTIC, went on air with a concert.
        Hartford Seminary (founded 1833) moved into new buildings on Elizabeth Street.

1925   Frederick Rentschler and George Mead perfected first air-cooled aircraft engine, thus founding Pratt & Whitney Aircraft.

1926   Christopher Columbus monument dedicated.
        New St. Ann's Church finished, Hartford's oldest French-speaking parish (1889).
        Vulcan Radiator produced first baseboard radiators.
1927   Children's Museum founded—fifth of its kind in the nation, now the Science Center of Connecticut.
        Charles A. Lindbergh visited city, first stop on his triumphant country-wide tour.
1929   Hartford joined Metropolitan District Commission.
1930   Bushnell Memorial Hall opened.
        Polish National Home on Charter Oak Avenue built.
1931   Aetna Life & Casualty occupied its new office building, at 669 feet the largest colonial-style structure in the world.
1932   St. Joseph College for Women founded in West Hartford.
1933   Veeder Root developed first counter to register price and gallons for gasoline pumps.
        Following repeal of Prohibition, Hotel Heublein given first permit for sale of beer.
        Founding of Hartford College for Women.
1934   Buses replaced trolleys on Farmington Avenue.
        Founding of Hartford Federal Savings.
        Hartford Symphony gave first concert in Avery Memorial Auditorium.
1935   Hartford celebrated its Tercentenary.
1936   Hartford's greatest flood, causing over $7 million property loss.
        Hartford Foundation for Public Giving made its first grant to Watkinson Library.
1938   Hartford's first hurricane in 100 years.
1939   Dedication of Brainard Airport (built 1921) as second oldest municipal airport in the country.
1941   The city's 45-foot high dike completed, and the Park River enclosed in a conduit, over which the Whitehead Highway was built. Center span of new Charter Oak Bridge collapsed, killing 16 men.
        Formation of Connecticut Opera Association.
1942   Charter Oak Bridge opened.
1943   Creation of the first state Civil Rights Commission.
        Gray Manufacturing Company produced first production model radar set.
        Ætna Life & Casualty insured Manhattan Project, first coverage of atomic power.
1944   Circus fire in Hartford killed 168 persons, Hartford's worst disaster.
1947   Albert A. LaPointe developed first long-distance TV antenna.
1948   City manager form of government became effective, with Carleton F. Sharpe appointed first city manager.
1950   City of Hartford reached its population peak of 177,397.
1952   First Mormon chapel in New England constructed.
        Opening of Connecticut Regional Market in South Meadows.
1953   Professor Vernon Krieble invented Loctite sealant at Trinity College.
        Hottest day on record occurred September 2—101 degrees.

1955   Wallace Stevens, insurance executive, won Pulitzer prize for poetry.

Severe flooding in Hartford and suburbs.

1956   Travelers Weather Service started.

Dedication of new Emanuel Lutheran Church (organized 1889) on Capitol Avenue.

Burning of St. Joseph Cathedral resulted in $5 million loss.

1957   University of Hartford founded.

Opening of new Hartford Public Library building.

1958   Travelers Insurance first to offer women life insurance at lower rates than insurance for men.

1960   Ground broken for Constitution Plaza, financed by Travelers Insurance Companies, Hartford's first major urban renewal project.

80.2 inches of snow fell in the winter of 1960-1961.

For first time number of employees in service businesses (including government) exceeded the number employed in manufacturing.

1961   Fire at Hartford Hospital killed 16 persons.

First commercial turbo-fan jet engine developed by Pratt & Whitney Aircraft.

1962   Connecticut Public Television began operations.

Connecticut Natural Gas first public utility to provide a central downtown area with both steam in winter and chilled water for air-conditioning in summer.

1963   Completion of Phoenix Mutual's new home office, the "boat building," first two-sided office structure in the world.

Hartford Electric Light first to use a Pratt & Whitney jet engine for emergency power generation.

1964   Founding of Hartford Stage Company.

Creation of United Bank & Trust Company from three smaller banks.

1965   Connecticut's new constitution drafted at Old State House.

1967   Opening of Greater Hartford Community College.

Formation of Center City Churches to serve the elderly and needy downtown.

Antonina P. Uccello became the city's first woman mayor.

1969   Society for Savings celebrated its 150th anniversary.

1970   Puerto Rican community established Templo Fe, an Assemblies of God church.

1971   Butler-McCook homestead, built in 1782, the last surviving 18th century house in Hartford, became headquarters of Antiquarian & Landmarks Society.

Greater Hartford Arts Council organized.

Hartford Graduate Center moved into new building on Windsor Street.

1972   Hartford Ballet founded.

1973   Dedication of Alexander Calder's Stegosaurus on Burr Mall.

Organization of Hartford Architecture Conservancy.

1974   Completion of One Financial Plaza, the "gold building," headquarters of United Technologies.

1975   Opening of Hartford Civic Center, financed by Aetna Life & Casualty.

First heliport on a Connecticut building at One Financial Plaza.

BELOW,
"Yankee Division, Welcome Home!"
102nd Infantry and 101st Machine
Gun Battalions on South Lawn of
Capitol. April 30, 1919.

1976	General Pulaski monument dedicated.
1977	Hartford Stage Company's new theater opened on Church Street.
1977	Carl Andre's controversial Stone Field Sculpture mounted on Gold Street.
1978	Collapse of Civic Center roof.
1979	New headquarters of Metropolitan District Commission dedicated.
1980	Riverfront Recapture, Inc. organized.
1981	Hartford elected its first black mayor, Thirman Milner. One-third of the 143,000 persons now employed within the city work for finance, insurance and real estate companies. Formation of Bushnell Park Foundation to renovate the park.
1983	Completion of CityPlace, 36 stories, the tallest building in Connecticut.
1984	Formation of Ancient Burying Ground Association.

"Yankee Division, Welcome Home!" 102nd Infantry and 101st Machine Gun Battalions on South Lawn of Capitol. April 30, 1919.

Foreign-Born in the Population of Hartford

United States Census—1860 to 1930, inclusive

Nationalities	1860	1870	1880	1890	1900	1910	1920	1930
Armenian	—	—	—	—	—	—	297	500
Austrian	—	20	15	104	664	1,865	919	677
Belgian	—	1	2	14	21	20	17	—
Canadian	179	396	481	815	1,309	1,332	1,532	2,132
Can. French	—	—	—	—	781	792	857	3,739
Danish	—	13	40	272	506	593	619	580
English	702	789	995	1,300	1,634	1,656	2,051	1,882
French	46	92	46	81	150	150	215	167
German	1,130	1,458	1,422	2,140	2,700	2,414	1,820	1,867
Greek	—	2	—	—	6	53	321	423
Hungarian	—	15	4	7	95	328	272	179
Irish	6,432	7,438	6,841	7,613	8,076	7,049	6,116	5,276
Italian	—	23	82	350	1,962	4,521	7,101	8,843
Lithuanian	—	—	—	—	—	—	1,260	1,593
Polish	—	17	19	19	506	1,656	4,880	5,236
Romanian	—	—	—	—	146	312	347	
Russian	—	5	4	492	2,260	6,847	7,864	5,830
Scotch	161	359	366	499	689	759	937	1,290
Swedish	—	16	72	515	1,714	2,185	2,315	2,161
	8,650	10,644	10,389	14,221	23,219	32,532	39,740	42,375

Courtesy of The Mitchell House, Inc. There were other "hidden minorities" too few to be included.

Population of Hartford and Suburbs

Date	Hartford	W. Hartford	E. Hartford	Windsor	Wethersfield	Enfield	Avon	Simsbury	Bloomfield	Newington
1820	6,901	—	3,373	3,008	3,825	2,065	—	1,954	—	—
1830	9,789	—	2,237	3,220	3,853	2,129	1,025	2,221	—	—
1840	12,793	—	2,389	2,283	3,824	2,648	1,001	1,895	986	—
1850	13,555	—	2,497	3,294	2,523	4,460	995	2,737	1,412	—
1860	29,152	1,296	2,951	3,865	2,705	4,997	1,059	2,410	1,401	—
1870	37,743	1,533	3,007	2,783	2,693	6,322	987	2,051	1,473	—
1880	42,551	1,828	3,500	3,052	2,173	6,755	1,057	1,830	1,346	934
1890	53,230	1,930	4,455	2,954	2,271	7,199	1,182	1,874	1,308	953
1900	79,850	3,186	6,406	3,614	2,637	6,699	1,302	2,094	1,513	1,041
1910	98,915	4,808	8,138	4,178	3,148	9,719	1,377	2,537	1,821	1,689
1920	138,036	8,854	11,648	5,620	4,342	11,719	1,534	2,958	2,394	2,381
1930	164,072	24,941	17,125	8,290	7,512	13,404	1,738	3,625	3,247	4,572
1940	166,267	33,776	18,615	10,065	9,644	13,561	2,258	3,941	4,309	5,449
1950	177,397	44,402	19,933	11,833	12,533	15,464	3,171	4,822	5,746	9,110
1960	162,178	62,382	43,977	19,467	20,561	31,464	5,273	10,138	13,613	17,664
1970	158,017	68,031	57,583	22,502	26,662	46,189	8,352	17,475	18,301	26,037
1980	136,392	61,301	52,563	25,204	26,013	42,695	11,201	21,161	18,608	28,841

	Hartford	Nine Suburbs
1820	6,901	14,225
1870	37,743	20,849
1920	138,036	50,450
1950	177,397	127,014
1960	162,178	226,539
1970	158,017	291,132
1980	136,392	287,589

Figures taken from the Connecticut State Register & Manual

Hartford Population in 1980

Total:		136,392

By Race

White	—	68,603
Black	—	46,186
American Indian	—	265
Asian Indian	—	261
Vietnamese	—	219
Chinese	—	160
Filipino	—	87
Korean	—	72
Japanese	—	36
Hawaiian/Samoan	—	14
Eskimos & Aleuts	—	11
Other	—	20,478

Spanish Origin

Puerto Rican	—	24,615
Cuban	—	681
Mexican	—	315
Other	—	2,287

Selected Ancestry Groups

Italian	—	10,141
Irish	—	5,406
Polish	—	4,995
French	—	4,477
Portuguese	—	4,018
English	—	4,006
German	—	1,595
Russian	—	1,035
Hungarian	—	247
Dutch	—	91
Norwegian	—	19

*Connecticut: 1980 Census of Population

For Further Reading

Andrews, Kenneth R. *Nook Farm, Mark Twain's Hartford Circle.* Cambridge, Mass.: Harvard University Press, 1950.

Barber, John Warner. *Connecticut Historical Collections.* New Haven: 1836.

Chapman, Helen P. *My Hartford in The Nineteenth Century.* Hartford: Edwin V. Mitchell, 1928.

Close, F. Perry. *History of Hartford Streets.* Hartford: Connecticut Historical Society, 1969.

Coote, Albert W. *Four Vintage Decades,* Hartford: Huntington, 1970.

Delaney, Edmund. *The Connecticut River.* Chester, Conn.: Globe-Pequot Press, 1983.

Erving, Henry W. *Connecticut River Banking Company.* Hartford: 1926.

Faude, Wilson H. and Friedland, Joan. *Connecticut First.* Old Saybrook: Peregrine Press, 1985.

Grant, Ellsworth S. *The Colt Legacy.* Providence, R.I.: Mowbray Company, 1982.

Grant, Ellsworth S. *The Club on Prospect Street,* Hartford: The Hartford Club, 1984.

Grant, Marion H. *In & About Hartford; Tours & Tales.* Hartford: Connecticut Historical Society, 1978.

McNulty, John Bard. *Older Than The Nation.* Chester, Conn.: Globe-Pequot Press, 1964.

Shepard, Odell. *Connecticut Past & Present.* New York: Alfred A. Knopf, 1939.

Trumbull, J. Hammond. *Memorial History of Hartford County.* Boston: Edward L. Osgood, 1886.

Van Dusen, Albert E. *Connecticut.* New York: Random House, 1961.

Weaver, Glenn. *Hartford, An Illustrated History of Connecticut's Capital.* Woodlands, CA: Windsor Publications, 1982.

Hartford, Connecticut. Hartford: Hartford Board of Trade, 1889.

The Main Stream of Connecticut. Hartford: Connecticut Historical Society Catalogue, 1981.

Picture Credits

Chapter 1
p. 9 *Miniature of Noah Webster:* Courtesy of the Litchfield Historical Society
p. 18 *Votes for Women parade:* From a private collection
p. 21 *John M. Bailey:* Courtesy of the Bailey family
p. 22 *Antonina P. Uccello:* From a private collection
p. 23 *Municipal Building:* From a private collection

Chapter 2
p. 25 BOTTOM: *Captain John Barnard:* From a private collection
p. 26 TOP: *A Yankee peddler:* From a private collection
p. 26 BOTTOM: *Poling a flatboat:* From a private collection
p. 28 *The "Oliver Ellsworth":* The Mariners' Museum, Newport News, VA.
p. 28 *The steamboat "Barnet":* From a private collection
p. 30 *United Technologies helicopter lands on top of Gold building:* Courtesy of United Technologies
p. 32 *Hartford Yacht Club:* From a private collection
p. 33 *Boating on Connecticut River, c. 1900:* From a private collection
p. 36 *Capitol Avenue:* Courtesy of the Hartford Collection, The Hartford Public Library

Chapter 3
p. 39 *Colonel Jeremiah Wadsworth and his son Daniel:* Courtesy Wadsworth Atheneum, Hartford
p. 40 *Society for Savings, 1834:* Courtesy of The Society for Savings
p. 41 *Society for Savings Headquarters on Pratt Street:* Photo by Charles Reich
p. 44 *Travelers Tower, Hartford, Dec. 1940:* Archive, The Travelers Companies

Chapter 4
p. 48 *Charles E. Billings in Uniform of Colt Band:* From a private collection
p. 50 *Samuel Colt:* From a private collection
p. 51 TOP: *Christopher Spencer:* Courtesy of Richard W. Forbes
p. 52 *George J. Mead, Frederick B. Rentschler, etc. inspect 1000th Wasp engine:* United Technologies Archive

Chapter 5
p. 63 *Rev. John Brady:* Courtesy of Archives, Archdiocese of Hartford.
p. 64 ABOVE: *The Rev. Dr. James W. C. Pennington:* Stowe-Day Foundation, Hartford, Connecticut
p. 64 BELOW: *Harriet Beecher Stowe:* Stowe-Day Foundation, Hartford, Connecticut.
p. 67 *St. Lucia Festival:* Courtesy of Emanuel Lutheran Church
p. 69 *Gideon Welles:* Courtesy of The Hartford Public Library
p. 70 *The French Social Club:* Photo by Robert J. Bitondi (via CHS)
p. 72 ABOVE: *Italian mother:* From a private collection
p. 73 ABOVE: *Sts. Cyril & Methodius Church:* Photo by Robert J. Bitondi (via CHS)
p. 73 ABOVE RIGHT: *Polish National Home:* From a private collection
p. 75 ABOVE: *Katharine Houghton Hepburn & family:* From a private collection
p. 75 RIGHT: *Suffrage Headquarters on Pratt Street:* Courtesy of the Hartford Collection, The Hartford Public Library
p. 76 RIGHT: *Health clinic for poor children:* Courtesy of Mitchell House
p. 78 ABOVE RIGHT: *Rev. Walter H. Gray:* From a private collection

NOTE: All pictures not listed on this sheet are from, and courtesy of The Connecticut Historical Society.

NOTE: All pictures not listed on this sheet are from and courtesy of The Connecticut Historical Society.

Acknowledgments

We wish first to express our thanks to the Society for Savings for their cooperation and financial assistance in making possible publication of *The City of Hartford*. The groundwork was laid four years ago when the Society asked us to undertake an update of *Passbook,* the bank's 150th anniversary history that we wrote in 1969. The project, however, evolved into a new history of the city to appear during its 350th anniversary. Many of the pictures used in *Passbook* have been replicated. Thus, to Elliott C. Miller, president, and to Robert W. Beggs Jr., vice-president of corporate communications, we are indebted for the opportunity to reinterpret the fascinating history of this old, yet very new metropolis.

The resources of the Connecticut Historical Society have been indispensable—not merely its extensive collections of prints and photographs, but the unstinting assistance and advice of Christopher P. Bickford, director; Kate D. Steinway, curator of prints and photographs, and her assistant Paige A. Savery; Robert J. Bitondi, staff photographer; Diana McCain, public information officer, and Frances Hoxie, who prepared the index. Grace Martin edited the manuscript.

In addition, Beverly Laughlin of the Hartford Public Library, the *Hartford Courant* and several corporations have been most generous in allowing us to draw from their photographic archives. We also want to recognize Charles Reich, who was responsible for all of the modern photographs in the chapter "Then and Now."

Finally, as persons not easily pleased when it comes to book design, we have nothing but the greatest admiration for the inspired work of the William Wondriska Associates Inc. and, in particular, Ann O'Brien.

Marion and Ellsworth Grant
July, 1986

About The Authors

Marion and Ellsworth Grant have, over the past 20 years, written numerous articles and books on Connecticut history. In 1969 they collaborated on a history of Society for Savings called *Passbook to a Proud Past & a Promising Future* on the occasion of its 150th anniversary. Marion's popular guidebook, *In & About Hartford,* published by the Connecticut Historical Society, has gone through several editions. Additionally, she was the author of *The Fenwick Story, The Internal Machines of Saybrook's David Bushnell, The Hart Dynasty of Saybrook* and *Fort Saybrook.*

Besides the many documentary films he has produced about Connecticut, Ellsworth has written *Yankee Dreamers & Doers, The Colt Legacy, Drop By Drop . . . The Loctite Story, Stanadyne* and *The Club on Prospect Street.*

Index

Design : Ann O'Brien
          Wondriska Associates
Type : Eastern Typesetting
Printing: Mark Burton Inc.